PRAISE FOR
BURNING WOMAN

Lucy Pearce has given voice to what a generation of women are feeling and burning to express. This book is filled with our collective calling, and inspires women to burn with our wild, fierce wisdom and creativity, and to push forwards to fully occupy our equality.

I celebrate this book and celebrate and acknowledge Lucy Pearce as a wise, wild and courageous woman who has written a very important book of our time. A must-read for all women! A life-changing book that fills the reader with a burning passion and desire for change!

Glennie Kindred, author and illustrator of eleven books on celebrating the Earth and ourselves

Burning Woman is a passionate call to wake up both to our present reality and to entrance ourselves to the remembrance of our power. Lucy's prose is poetic, raw and dances on the edge of outrageous — where outrageous means to defy what we have been taught and have accepted to our detriment. I am proud to call myself a burning woman...

Jane Meredith, author of
Journey to the Dark Goddess* and *Circle of Eight: Creating Magic for Your Place on Earth

Lucy H. Pearce's Burning Woman carries the torch of the sacred Feminine into the dark corners of women's unexpressed and unfulfilled desire and power. She dares us to burn down that which does not serve life, to use our fire to transform the world.

Oriah 'Mountain Dreamer' House

Gripping, grounded, affirming and real. I wish I could gift every girl and woman I know a copy of this book. We deserve more than a bland flat surface description of ourselves as women — or airy fairy feminine metaphors—we are vast beyond measure and complex and we are indeed burning.

Clare Campbell, artist and creative activist,
founder of Big Love Sista CIC and Wild Woman

Lucy Pearce is a gifted writer, a gentle wayshower, and a fierce pioneer in these times of global transformation. In her new book, she reveals potent information to the woman reader, reminding her of her true heritage, kindling the fire within, to more fully claim our truth and embody it in our daily lives. This knowledge has been hidden from us, and we are now ready to receive it. This book is a true gift and, if you are a woman ripe for transformation, it can fan the inner flames, sparking you to own that fire and let it burn all that is false within you, revealing the power that was yours all along. Every woman should read this book! Thank you Lucy!

Bethany Webster, Healing the Mother Wound

In an era when Western feminism seems too often about loudly celebrating woman as victim, this is a refreshing book. Yes, sometimes we get burned, but allowing the fire to fuel our strength is a far more intelligent response. Lucy's vibrant words are a sound reminder, and a joy to read.

Emma Restall Orr, author of *Kissing the Hag*

This book is initiation by ignition. Lucy Pearce has reached into the hearth of womanhood, pulled out the hottest coals, and given us Burning Woman, a text and feminine archetype channelled just for these times. Within these pages, she dares to ask and answer fundamental questions about feminine power – why are we afraid of it? How can we claim it? What is at risk if we do? What is at risk if we DON'T? With torch held high, Burning Woman carries us across the threshold of inquiry and fear, guiding us toward our own flame of inner truth. If you're no longer willing or able to play it safe, if you're aching to burn bright, if you're already dancing in the fire, read this book and source the fuel of Burning Women from every time, everywhere.

Autumn Weaver and Baraka Elihu,
Birthing Ourselves into Being

Lucy burns a hole right through the fabric of our societal programming and identifies the true source of why even the most empowered women attempt to walk in their power only to hold back from fully stepping into it. Heal the Burning Woman and we'll see a radical shift and healing in every aspect of our world.

Suzanne Mathis McQueen, author of *4 Seasons in 4 Weeks*

Burning Woman is a marvellous, impassioned, emotional read. This book will root you back to your woman power and inspire you to rise up with other burning women to change the world. I encourage you to read Burning Woman TODAY! The world needs our collective female flames right NOW. Thank you Lucy Pearce for this tremendous book.

Trista Hendren, author of *The Girl God* series

Are you a woman who yearns for something more? Do you feel the seed of a hot, rebel, spirit hidden inside somewhere? A wildness you're not sure how to set free? With Burning Woman, author Lucy Pearce brings us a living, breathing manifesto for real women. A burning hot antidote to the vague and cool tones of the endless wave of self-help and development books on the market. Digging deep into herstory, showing us the roots of our blocks and fears, sharing her own burning story, Lucy blazes the way for every woman to free the burning soul within. Take a deep breath and dive in.

Awen Clement, founder MoonWise Woman

BURNING WOMAN

Lucy H. Pearce

WOMANCRAFT PUBLISHING

Typeset and design by Lucent Word, Co. Cork, Ireland
Cover art by Robin Lea Quinlivan

Extended quotations used with the express permission of their authors.

Published by Womancraft Publishing, 2016
www.womancraftpublishing.com

ISBN: 978-1-910559-161 (Paperback)
ISBN: 978-1-910559-178 (ebook)

A percentage of Womancraft Publishing profits are invested back into the environment reforesting the tropics (via TreeSisters) and forward into the community: providing books for girls in developing countries, and affordable libraries for red tents and women's groups around the world.

Womancraft Publishing is committed to sharing powerful new women's voices, through a collaborative publishing process. We are proud to midwife this work, however the story, the experiences and the words are the author's alone.

For you, Burning Woman,
may the fire within you
burn stronger than the flames without.

BY THE SAME AUTHOR

Full Circle Health; integrated health charting for women

Moon Time: harness the ever-changing energy of your menstrual cycle

The Rainbow Way: cultivating creativity in the midst of motherhood

Moods of Motherhood: the inner journey of mothering

Reaching for the Moon: a girl's guide to her cycles

CONTRIBUTOR TO...

If Women Rose Rooted: The Power of the Celtic Woman —Sharon Blackie (September Publishing, 2016)

Wild + Precious: The Best of Wild Sister Magazine —Jen Saunders (Wild Sister, 2014)

Tiny Buddha's Guide to Loving Yourself—Lori Deschene (Hay House, 2013)

Roots: Where Food Comes From, and Where It Takes Us (BlogHer, 2013)

Earth Pathways Diary (2011–2017)

Musings on Mothering: An Anthology of Art, Poetry and Prose —Teika Bellamy (Mother's Milk Books, 2012)

Note to Self: The Secret to Becoming Your Own Best Friend — Jo MacDonald (2012)

CONTENTS

She woke up one day and decided to set her life on fire; to go up in flames if necessary. To really live the life she was born to live.

Lynn Bartle

ACKNOWLEDGEMENTS

Burning Woman is a big book. This is the feedback I have had from each of my treasured early readers. Big in every way. It ranges far and wide in ideas and literary form, and connects many dots which I have not seen connected before. Be warned that it is also an embodied alchemical process. It holds great power, which at many times I doubted I could birth.

It began as seeds of fire I gathered over many years. Each time I shared a seed, it seemed to start a wildfire of recognition amongst the women that witnessed it. I knew I was onto something.

But I did not know if I dared to write it: it was too big, too powerful and I felt too small. This book has challenged me at every turn to stand in my own authority. I am still standing. And shaking. Humbled and grateful for its medicine. It has made me braver.

I want to express my deep gratitude to all those who have shown such courage and vision in their fields, whose work my own borrows from and builds on: Barbara Ann Brennan, Clarissa Pinkola Estés, Sera Beak, Brené Brown, Mary Daly, Ina May Gaskin, Jennifer Louden, Naomi Lowinsky, Maureen Murdock, Vicki Noble, Emma Restall Orr, Julia Penelope, Starhawk, Marion Woodman, Pat Allen, Baraka Elihu and Autumn Weaver, Sigmund Freud, C.G. Jung, Nietzsche, Charles Eisenstein, Peter Levine and Clark Strand... your words have shone light on the dark places of my soul.

It is, as always, my honour and pleasure to weave the words of many women to make a mightier tapestry of rich perspectives than my lone voice could ever manage. I want to pay tribute to the choir of Burning Women who join me in this book: Shiloh Sophia McCloud, Bethany Webster, Isabel Abbott, Julie Daley, Antonia Rothschild, Lucy Pierce, Sarah Durham Wilson, Molly Remer and ALisa Starkweather—though we have never met, it feels as though we are working from the same source, in sync, I am grateful for your ever-generous spirits. And to my first Womancraft authors, Nicole Schwab, Melia Keeton-Digby and Eila Kundrie Carrico whose words have shaped me as I have shaped them. And Matt Licata whose words washed my way on the shores of Facebook one day, whose spirit is tangible, a Burning Man of deep gentleness.

To my circles of sisters: The East Cork Red Tent, that unwittingly started this whole journey; my women's group who have recently regathered, we have travelled more than seven years together, and you are my soft space to fall; to my revolutionary women in my Be Your Own Publisher Facebook group, and Bethany Webster's incredible crew of women on the Healing the Mother Wound course who have truly midwived me during the last stages of writing this book. For your wisdom, courage and sisterhood on the journey, thank you.

My husband, Patrick Treacy, who has consistently given me the space and support I need to burn brightly. And the arms to retreat to when I have been burned or burn out.

Jackie Stewart, Awen Clement, Lou Hayden, Leigh Millar, Mary Tighe and my sister, Mirin Mooney, each of whom have walked the path of this book by my side, in ceremony, in powerful conversations. For reading early drafts, cheering me on my way, being brave enough to dive deep with me and for holding me when I wobbled—thank you.

Tracy Evans, my doula and midwife, the seer of my soul, who hears each of my creative book babies into being through her deep listening, powerful space-holding and complete belief in me. Without her I would not be the me I am. We mirror each other's souls and teach and learn so much through our deep friendship. I am so very grateful for her presence in my life and her insight into this work.

And finally my children, that they may burn with their own passions, and fight different battles to us. They inspire me to act now to prevent the world burning up in the flames of fossil fuels and patriarchy, so they may have their chance to live brightly in peace on this beautiful Earth.

INVITATION

The Dalai Lama said,
"The world will be saved by the Western woman,"
and I agree, she might just be a burning world's last chance. But
before she saves the world, she has to save herself. So how?
How do we heal ourselves to heal the world?
Sarah Durham Wilson, DoItGirl.com

For years I have joked with my women's circle that we would dance around a bonfire. Naked.

It is a running joke that come the next full moon or summer solstice we'll all strip off and dance naked. We tease our husbands that we will enact this ultimate cliché which a gathering of women arouses: the naked circle of witches, wild women or radical feminist empowerment groups. But most of us, myself included, are quite reserved and not ones for dancing naked in public. But it doesn't stop us talking about it, eyes sparkling with a daring we're not sure we really possess in the flesh.

The more I think about it, the more I see it as our subconscious desires expressing themselves.

Dancing naked around a bonfire is a powerful metaphor: a longing to be naked, authentic, vulnerable in our own skins. A longing to be ourselves: feminine and free, dancing together... and at the same time alone. The rhythm pulsing through us. The beat moving us. The fire our elemental centre-point, lighting our steps, burning away our anxieties and burdens.

Rooting us in ourselves, in sisterhood, in the Earth.

Our conventional selves snigger at the idea of waggling our boobs in the moonlight, thighs wobbling in the chill night air. What would people think? What would they say if they knew? Would the neighbours see us? Would the other women stare at me and judge me for my imperfect body? How could I ever look my friend in the eye again once I had seen her muff? Our cheeks burn with shame at the thought. Every box is ticked: something outside of our cultural comfort zone, body issues, women together — must be lesbians, witches, crazy, mad — all the labels that over the years have been successfully used to keep women down, shut us up, get us back in line.

The fire which burns outside is still greater, for most of us, than the one that burns within. And so we keep our clothes on, laugh away the discomfort, and say, with sadness and determination: "Next year! We'll do it next year." But we never do.

This book is for you, dearest woman if you long to be more powerful and courageous, and know that now is the time to step into your own skin and be seen.

Will you come and dance around the bonfire with me? Do you dare to face down the stereotypes and the shame? Do you have the courage to dance to your own tune and be witnessed? Do you dare to burn bright with your own inner flame visible to all?

Let yourself be embraced by the powerful sisterhood within these pages. Warm your soul on their burning words. Dare to venture into the sweet dark and bitter cold and be cradled beneath the bare trees, as you gather with friends to watch the flames lick and dance, the sparks fly. Feel the sense of danger and delight, the warmth on your hands and face and belly as the fire grows brighter.

Let us find a way for the fire within to overcome the fire without.

We are living in burning times and they call for Burning Women. This is our time to come out of the shadows and burn brightly. Let's throw off our clothes and dance round the fire together.

This book is a wake-up call to the Burning Woman within you. A remembering through words, visions, poems and practices, an invitation to reinhabit your powerful body. It contains the prayers and petitions of a hundred voices, to awaken the Burning Woman within each of us, to call up our courage to step into her. It is a hymn to the powerful woman. A love letter to the crazy woman, the mad one, the witch, the hag. An invitation to the creative woman: the dancer, the poet, the artist. A call to arms for the activist, the strident woman, the playful trickster. It is an embrace of the passionate woman and the wild mother. It is written for every woman who follows her own spirit, who dares to put herself first. She who shouts in the face of authority and follows her heart not their God. She who dares to give voice to what is inside her, who shakes things up and burns them down. She who quakes with rage and rolls with laughter, who moans with pleasure and wants more. She for whom every piece of life needs to have the marrow of its bones sucked, who dances naked, and eats with her fingers. She who stamps and says no. She who stands in the doorway and will not let them in. She who opens her legs and dives into her juices with delight. She who dares. She who does what they say cannot be done, must not be done. She who tries and fails. She who does it her way. She who longs to walk topless in the sunshine and dance naked in the moonlight.

It is for her, and all of us, who long to be more like her wherever on the path we may be. We who have sniffed the smoke as she walked past our door one hot summer afternoon and thought, *I long to burn, but I mustn't. I'm too afraid, too old, too young, too busy. I don't know how. I'd lose my job, my husband would divorce me, my mother would disown me, my friends would laugh. . .*

This is for you, dearest one,

You are more powerful than you dare believe.

This is for you, Burning Woman. . .

ARISE!

1

BURNING WOMAN

We dare not talk of the darkness, for fear it will infect us.
We dare not talk of the fire, for fear it will destroy us.
And so we live in the half-light,
Like our mothers before us.

Come to the fire,
Feel it warm your skin.
Come to the fire,
Feel it burn in your belly,
Shine out through your eyes.
Come dance in the fire,
Let it fuel your prayers.

This book is for all women who burn with passion. Have been burned by shame. And in other places, at other times would have been burned alive for what they do and who they are.

It is written for every woman who has struggled with expressing herself. Every woman filled with burning questions, who longed to give voice to the ideas within her, but was too scared by what might happen if she did. It is dedicated to every woman who is in the process of stepping into her power. And every single woman who has been burned when she did.

In my work with hundreds of women over the past few years a theme has emerged: women's desperate, unquenchable desire to step into their power, countered by the fear of what will happen if they do. The longing to express the riches inside them, wrestling with the deep terror of being burned by the judgement, hatred or rejection of strangers or loved ones if they do.

This fear of being burned is an oddly female one. It is a fear which keeps us small and scared... but seemingly safe. From the outside this can seem like an overreaction. Both the need, and the fear. But women, it seems, have an innate knowing of what it means to burn... and be burned. They know the dangers in their bones. And it makes them wary.

In the words of one woman:

"I have worked on a fear of being me for so long — an abject terror that being me would equal death."

I identify completely.

Because I too have learned that who I am, what I do, is dangerous.

Just a couple of months before the idea for this book came to me in full force I had what I can only call a waking dream. I was standing in the kitchen, when suddenly I realised I could burn for my work.

The agony of this almost strangled me from within. I realised I could stand to lose everything — my reputation, my community, my beloved husband, my precious children — simply for doing the work that I burn to do.

About a year before I had had an email, out of the blue, from a woman who warned me that I could be on the radar of the powers-that-be. She had been hunted out of Ireland, she said, tried at a secret court, found guilty of witchcraft. And she was not as visible as I was. My head swam. What were the consequences of doing my women's work in a world that felt threatened by it? I tried to put her warnings aside as the paranoid ramblings of a crazy lady.

But this fear — whether a feeling in our bones, or a

substantiated threat from outside—keeps most of us caged and small.

I know. Because the women I work with tell me this. They tell me how trapped by terror they are; that their desire to create or speak out is submerged by fear. What is at the root of this, I wondered? And so, as I travelled from my own personal fear, to this more universal female experience of burning for our work or our creativity or sexuality, the seeds of this book were sown.

For almost a decade I have written words for women — in books and blogs and articles for magazines and newspapers. I have woven ceremonies and led groups, I have taught classes and talked and listened to women around the world. I know that there is a hunger, a yearning, right now. Many, many women can feel something stirring within, and they sense something stirring without. Something far bigger than just their desire to paint or write or start a blog or a business or a protest. There is a collective burning igniting within women. A deep need to tell our stories and be heard. A longing to heal past hurts and move beyond them, into something big and bold and fresh and new. Something is changing, we can sense it. And yet when we have this yearning, when we hear this calling, there is still the paralysing fear: *will I be burned alive?*

Over the past two months I have noticed something else amongst my Facebook communities: a rise in anger and frustration, the feeling that enough is enough. Enough of bitchy competitiveness amongst women, enough internet trolling, and misogynistic social media memes, enough rape threats, enough brutal acts of terrorism, enough bully boy tactics on the international political stage, enough austerity, enough exhausting ourselves trying to be everything to everyone.

We have had enough.

We are emerging from a sense of helpless, numb denial that nothing can be done, into a burning belief that something must be done... and the knowledge that each of us has to act in whatever way we can to help it come about. I have witnessed as women have stepped into their power — organising fundraisers and collections of supplies for refugees, starting or sharing petitions, leaving jobs and abusive relationships, starting businesses and new lives.

We are learning that we are the ones we have been waiting for: it is both thrilling and terrifying. We hear the call, but hold back, unsure as to what it might entail. We have received the invitation to step more fully into ourselves, but do not know if we dare to respond. We fear what comes next. We believe that in order to step into greater worldly power, we must be more powerful. But we don't know how.

And we have seen the lives of powerful women in the public eye enough to know that each step we take towards our truth, requires trial by fire — inner and outer — as we find the courage to face down the judgements and restrictions of others and embody ourselves more authentically. We can sense this, and it scares us. We don't know how to proceed, because the mainstream world does not acknowledge the winds of change that are making our noses twitch. And so we can feel alone, burned out, frustrated, and even a little crazy as we try to work with these massive energies that are shifting within us, and in the world outside.

INCENDIARY WORDS

Men often react to women's words — speaking and writing — as if they were acts of violence; sometimes men react to women's words with violence. So we lower our voices. Women whisper. Women apologize. Women shut up. Women trivialize what we know. Women shrink. Women pull back. Most women have experienced enough dominance from men — control, violence, insult, contempt — that no threat seems empty.
Andrea Dworkin, *Intercourse*

I must warn you that the ideas within these covers will be incendiary to many. This is a book of her(e)say which will contradict so much of the existing paradigm. It is strongly and proudly at variance with the established beliefs of his-story that we have been taught to unquestioningly accept and obey. Let me be very clear, that my intention is not to attack or shame any individual or their heartfelt personal belief. I honour our diversity of being and belief. To me, personal belief, where it does no harm to others, is sacred. What I do not hold sacred are the structures of power and dogma that have been unassailable for most of his-story, that have caused untold damage to individuals and cultures. It is at those that I am taking aim with my burning questions.

His-story has brought us here. But it cannot save us. His-story is burning us *all* alive. The temperatures are rising, ice caps are melting, sea levels are rising. These are the burning times. A time of systemic collapse. But within it is the spark of new life: the potential for paradigm shift is rich, ripe and ready. Now the phoenix of humanity can rise out of the flames of the old culture. Now is the time for the return of the Feminine into her full power, to work in partnership with a new, mature Masculine. Now is the time to give birth to a new world. The midwives are being summoned. Burning Women hear the call.

But not everyone wants a new world. Not by a long shot. Many are deeply invested in the old world model, or they feel trapped and powerless. Many even think that the revolutions have happened, and we are already inhabiting happily ever-after.

Just today I read a male supporter of home-grown Middle Eastern feminists (who had stormed a stage and bared their naked breasts in protest) chastise American women: "YOU are not oppressed. THESE women are oppressed." I have been chided like this too. Told, in no uncertain terms, that as a middle-class, cis-gendered, "hetero" white woman in a

European country in 2015 I have no idea about oppression, and any oppression I perceive is attention-seeking victimhood and lame excuses. *There is no burning*, I am told, *so shut your mouth, get back in your box and be grateful.*

Well, before I drop my head in deference, let's just recall the statistic that one in five American women is sexually assaulted at college,[i] that there are just 27 female world leaders in 197 countries.[ii] Or that the majority of world religions are ministered and led almost exclusively by men. When I was a child women priests did not exist, in any mainstream Christian church. In the Catholic church they still do not.

Enough of religion and politics already? How about business, then, where feminism has supposedly done its thing? But here the statistics are little better: just 14% of top executives in the US are female,[iii] in Japan this figure is just 3%. The leader in world gender equality, Norway, has just a third of women in top jobs.[iv] Across the board the pay gap has narrowed to a mere 19.1% in the UK, for men and women doing the same level of work. After 40 years of pay equality being enshrined in law.[v] It doesn't get any better in the arts, with only two women making Forbes' list of the top twenty earning actors in 2015, and whilst less than 3% of the artists in the Modern Art section of New York's Metropolitan Museum of Art are women, 83% of the nudes are female.[vi]

Yes, we're allowed to drive and attend sports events, unlike in Saudi Arabia, yes we can stand in law to defend ourselves, unlike in sharia law, yes we can receive an equal education without being shot or kidnapped, as in Pakistan and Nigeria. But equal in power and opportunity? Ha!

If you still believe that women and men currently enjoy full equality in our world, or that women's subjugation is divinely ordained, then either buckle up and prepare to be challenged. . . or go enjoy happily ever after, and pass this book on to the woman in your life with the wild look in her eyes. The one that burns with a passion she doesn't quite know how to access. The one whom darkness covers from time to time. The one who went out one night in the dark and lost her courage. The one who churns and struggles and rattles cages. The one who has lost her mother, lost herself. The one who is losing her faith. The one who dreams of revolution. The one who has been burned deep by shame. The one who longs for more.

FIRE AND THE FEMININE

Many non-Western traditions state that feminine energy is about receiving. However most of us in the West have been taught that feminine energy is about giving.
Dr Eve Agee, *The Uterine Health Companion*

For too long women have been told they are like the moon, reflecting the glory of the sun. We are told that the feminine is receptive, watery, submissive, full of beauty not power.

In her book, *Shakti Woman*, Vicki Noble relates an epiphany about this: "The Feminine to [my husband] was related to the planet Neptune and the elusive watery element and seemed from my perspective to be weak, insubstantial, and conveniently not really there. The Jungian view of the 'anima' [inner feminine] as vacuous and seductive, alluring yet forever unattainable, was offensive to my feminist consciousness. 'If that is the Feminine,' I screamed at him, 'then what am I?!' The Feminine, in my version, was fiery and substantial, taking up real space with her real expression of self and demanding to be encountered rather than imagined."

I am with her. Whilst I have parts of me that are reflective and watery, I have lots of fire in my soul too. I, and multitudes of other women, were not made to be passive and submissive as our culture has taught us for most of history. We burn. Our experience of the Feminine is not confined to water and air: we are consumed with fire.

Fire is not a purely Masculine realm. Nor is water a Feminine domain. We each have access to both elements. We each have the Masculine and Feminine within us. But our culture has set one against the other. And kept the fire from our hands.

It is time for us reclaim Feminine fire. Expressed by women. In women's ways.

Have we not done that already? you ask. Feminism has happened. We are not 1950s housewives, trapped by the feminine mystique. We are not shrinking violets, bound by Victorian-era morals and corsets. We are modern women.

Yes, we are, but still we are party to moral codes so different to men, which aim to keep us obedient and submissive in subtle ways. It seems that however many times women rise, those women of fire who led the suffragettes and the waves of feminist movements, women as a whole are put back in their place. What happens to women of fire still in our culture? We get held to different standards, and we get burned.

*

I have watched in interest as women the world over have used metaphors of burning when they speak of power and passion: burning embers of passion, having their fingers burned, being incandescent with rage, smoke and mirrors. It seems to be a common vernacular, a shorthand amongst women, that needs no translation. It is barely a metaphor for those who burn, whether with passion or shame: the burning is literal.

As one of the four elements, fire is a primal building block of the world and evokes deep feelings, emotional and physical. Transformative by its very nature, it is both creative and destructive. Powerful, yet insubstantial, fire is both there and not. The flames flickering this way and that. Where are its edges? What is its form? It is always in flux.

I am a firm believer in the power of words to move energy

into matter and thought into action. Words help us to share our experiences and visions for a new reality. As Julia Penelope says, "the process of finding different ways to talk is a necessary prerequisite to reshaping what and how we think."

This book is full of burning words. Metaphors.

Metaphors invoke vivid emotional responses within us by taking simple language and weaving through powerful but familiar images and associations. These living images appear to have a direct access not only to our brains, but emotions, physical bodies and energy too, in a way that more technical, logical language does not. They provide keys to our unconscious, allowing access to previously inaccessible memories, ideas and power.

Our world is constructed from metaphors, woven from stories. We're told that "life's a bitch", and we're engaged in a "war of the sexes", we "play with fire" and "get burned", we have "fire in our bellies" or are "cold-hearted". We have become so used to these phrases that we treat them as incontrovertible truths. We fail to see the metaphors as just that. When we unpick the old patriarchal metaphors of war and domination at the seams, we realise that we have the power to create new metaphors in their place, to remake the world in our own image.

I believe that metaphor and archetype are keys to the transformation of consciousness. Each of my books is based on this understanding — the weaving of words with images and creative exercises to actualise real change within ourselves and our world.

What first appears to be a book, is in fact an initiation. As you read, I invite you to stay aware of your body and emotions, note the impact that the words and the ideas have on you internally. Feel where they inflame you, with passion or anger. See where they hit blockages or seed sparks. Because they will.

These are burning words.

Written for you, Burning Woman.

THE F WORD

How can we, women, who have been taught to be afraid of every little noise in the night, dare to imagine that we might destroy the world that men defend with their armies and their lives? How can we, women, who have no vivid memory of ourselves as heroes, imagine that we might succeed in building a revolutionary community? Where can we find the revolutionary courage to overcome our slave fear?

Sadly, we are as invisible to ourselves as we are to men. We learn to see with their eyes — and they are near blind. Our first task, as feminists, is to learn to see with our own eyes.
Andrea Dworkin

Burning Woman is a book of feminine power.

For years I would have run the other way, making puking noises, rather than pick up a book about the feminine. If that's you, I hear you.

Let's start our exploration right there: in the feminine — that which supposedly defines us as women, but which so many of us feel ambivalent about at best, but often hostile, detached or alienated from. The feminine stands for all that we have been taught to reject as deeply flawed or inconsequential: our mothers, ourselves, other women, nature... We have unconsciously imbibed the incessant patriarchal propaganda about the weak inferiority of the feminine, its inherent imperfection, its silliness and triviality.

We live in a culture that is only just, in very recent history, opening up to the possibility of women as equals. Ours is a culture that has been built, ruled and inherited from father to son — in heaven as on Earth. This is the patriarchy, literally meaning, "the rule of the father", a social system "in which males hold primary power, predominate in roles of political leadership, moral authority, social privilege and control of property; in the domain of the family, fathers or father-figures hold authority over women and children." [vii]

Ours is a culture in which the masculine is the norm. Both genders in our culture have learned to suppress signs of the feminine in order to survive and be accepted, which has led to a hyper-masculinised culture of men... and women. And we have been taught to "perform" the feminine in order to gain approval, sexual attraction and power. As women in Western culture we have been taught to value more masculine traits and denigrate, disregard or trivialise more typically feminine ways of being.

"The feminine" is usually shorthand for: beautiful, gentle, slim, restrained, non-confrontational, carefully cultivated, domesticated, emotional, girlish and weak. It is often a term of disparagement... because the feminine has been blacklisted. Most qualities deemed not masculine, or in any way pertaining to women, have been slighted, shamed or silenced. To do something like a girl is a pejorative statement.

Whilst women's options have undeniably increased in the modern world, *feminine* is still quite a small prison cell for the female soul. In our current economy, *feminine* is used to sell infantile tat at inflated prices to hungry, powerless women who long to be perfect enough to be acceptable and loved.

As a good damaged girl of the patriarchy, I have tried (and failed), at various points in my life to be feminine when I longed to fit in. I painted my walls peach and my nails pink and my face an odd beige. I curled my eyelashes in the desperate attempt to be acceptably feminine in the eyes of the world. I have tottered on heels and laughed politely at men's unfunny jokes, worn push-up bras and painful thongs, bitten my tongue and said no to dessert (well, maybe once) to be more feminine.

But really, I don't care. And I have a sense that what it means to be a woman is a whole lot bigger than having a pink Kitchen

Aid, a passion for shoes and pneumatic breasts. And I think you do to. But try talking about what the feminine really is, or what a woman is and you're going to get a whole lot of people hot under the collar. And not in a sexy way. I know, because it's my job, and people like to fling shit my way when I open my mouth to say things they don't like.

So it's no surprise that if people get worked up about what you mean by woman or feminine, they go bat-shit crazy when you mention the g word. Goddess. I have avoided it like the plague in my previous writing, because I know it is so deeply misunderstood. Both by many who claim to follow her and most who are riled by the notion of Her. The Feminine face of God isn't some vajazzled diva, nor the devil in disguise, but an awesome power source, the nature behind nature, the raw life force, the power behind our power.

But it's generally safer not to talk about Her.

You see, what I have discovered, writing books about women, for women, is that we have a lot of no-go areas. Not only subjects that we cannot, should not, must not talk about for fear of upsetting everyone, but also a lack of common language. We lack acceptable words for speaking about our bodies, our sexual experiences, spiritual experiences, maternal experiences. And so when someone dares to, and gets it wrong, what do we do? Oh yes, we burn her!

So please know that I'm not throwing these terms around lightly. And nor do I have any attachment to what you choose to call these things we'll be exploring. Or even if our beliefs diverge. But as we're working with words, then you need to know what I mean. I have to choose words to contain these ideas. But if certain words rankle with you, mentally replace them with those you feel more comfortable with whilst retaining the spirit and intention behind them. The right word holds the key to not only your basic comprehension, but also your deeper, somatic understanding.

So let's differentiate now by using a capital F. What I mean by *Feminine* here is the power of the life force shooting through a birthing mother; the gentleness of a woman breastfeeding her newborn; the passion, strength and vulnerability of a woman in orgasm; the connection of blood and steel of a woman with her sister; the fierceness of a woman defending her family.

The Feminine is your wild instinctive self, your core longing, your deepest life force. It is that which feels most true to you as a woman: uncultivated and raw. The Feminine is that which makes you alive and makes you burn. The Feminine is your passion: your expression of love, sexuality, creativity, relationship, beauty, devotion... through your female body and mind. The Feminine is the felt sense of acting in the world, based primarily in the body, rather than through the mind.

As an aside I'm aware that there are many who do not identify with their gender or the bodies they were born into. Body dysphoria is common in this modern world, commoner than we'd admit. Whatever gender we were assigned at birth, we all have both masculine and feminine energies and drives within us. And we're all born into a patriarchal culture which sees and shapes us differently into stunted, restricted versions of the full people we could be. So we're all doing the dance with learning to express them both authentically within our human bodies, but for some the struggle is harder.

Defining the Feminine is immediately problematic — it sets up a dichotomy with the Masculine. And in this world, we have a habit of making dichotomies into good and bad. Not so fast, if you're wanting some man-hating you've come to the wrong place. The masculinity we see running rampant in the patriarchal system is not the developed Masculine, but the defensive masculine, the immature, ego-based masculine trying to defend a man-made hierarchical order against chaos, nature and the Feminine.

The reality we are currently inhabiting is the shadowlands

where immature masculine and feminine are awaiting transformation into a creative partnership of their fully mature selves.

So here we are. We've learned how to live life on masculine terms, through our minds, with our feelings shut down. Men and women both. And the Feminine. . . well, her ass has been beaten and locked up, her tongue cut out, she has been stoned, shamed, tied to a stake and burned. Again and again. Over the course of a couple of thousand years. Around the world. And because we rather like staying alive, women and men have both learned to subdue their expression of the Feminine.

The Feminine has been demoted, defanged, disempowered. Her innate power—her sexuality and beauty, nurturing instinct and creativity — replaced with the safe imitations of it, done as performance, and always with reference to what is pleasing to the male gaze. We have been sold back the feminine with a small f, in lipstick tubes and powder puffs and fake boobs. At a high price.

But we say "enough!" We refuse to buy what they are selling any more. We are claiming our birthright, stepping into a mature Feminine power that we get to define for ourselves.

Where the feminine is pink,

The Feminine is

Blood red.

Fire red.

Burning hot.

A power to be reckoned with.

WOMEN AND POWER ... THE STORY SO FAR

The majority of the population in virtually all nation states is female and is forced by patriarchy to obey, be silent, and acquiesce which means that 'democracy' does not yet exist anywhere. What happens then when that majority refuses to obey?
Robin Morgan, *The Demon Lover*

Power.

Even the word burns with promise. . . and danger.

Power in our world is usually synonymous with money, status, material possessions, authority, politics. It is associated with big guns, big muscles, grand titles, silly hats, tall towers . . . oh, and men.

Power in all its forms has been historically considered the domain of the masculine. And for most of history the only way a woman could gain power or money was by offering her body in some sort of exchange for it: through marriage, servitude, childbirth, sexual favours. . . Power was given, and it could be taken away, without warning. A woman's own innate power was denied, scorned or prohibited: by God, and law, and man, her role was to demure, submit to and obey the powers that be. Or be punished

Let us look a little closer at the structure of patriarchal power which has dominated our culture for thousands of years. We are so familiar with it, that it's often hard to see it for what it is.

Look around you. All the major civilizations are represented by stone phalluses: temples with ornate columns, church steeples, vertiginous glass sky scrapers and pyramids. From the desert pyramids of Egypt and the jungle pyramids of the Mayans, through the pyramid with the all-seeing eye on the back of every dollar bill: they have been the dominant symbol of masculine order and control.

The power we have experienced so far in our lives on Earth

is man-made power. The power of the pyramid with God the Father at the top, his kings and priests below him and then women in their "rightful place" further down. This patriarchal model of power has been refined and violently imposed as "divine right" over a couple of millennia, through states, churches, homes, asylums, torture chambers, bed chambers and jail cells, until the majority have learned to submit. It has been enforced through laws and threats and free trade treaties and rape and genocide.

> *Patriarchy is a political-social system that insists that males are inherently dominating, superior to everything and everyone deemed weak, especially females, and endowed with the right to dominate and rule over the weak and to maintain that dominance through various forms of psychological terrorism and violence...*
> **bell hooks**

But the pyramidal paradigm of power is already crumbling. The fallacy of phallocratic rule is being exposed. The old stories can no longer support it, they are being ripped away and overwritten. The patriarchy is akin to the Wizard of Oz —hidden behind his curtain, projecting power through smoke and mirrors —the time has come to pull the curtain aside and reveal his true impotence.

THREADS OF POWER

> *It is not power that corrupts, but fear. Fear of losing power corrupts those who wield it and fear of the scourge of power corrupts those who are subject to it.*
> **Aung San Suu Kyi**

This word *power*, it is slippery and complex, with layers of meaning. What do I mean by power?

I mean political and cultural power — the ability to make decisions, to express ourselves and contribute meaningfully to our culture.

I mean economic power — the right and ability to own and use money, status and possessions as a mature adult.

I mean spiritual power — the right and ability to commune with our interpretation of the sacred in our own way.

I mean creative power — the ability to vision and create our own visions of reality.

I mean biological power — health and wellbeing, the life force energy.

I mean power as in physical strength — the sovereignty over one's own physical body.

I mean personal power — the right of an individual to fully inhabit their life and express their being (in ways that do no harm) without fear.

When we are starting out these might seem like a load of disparate strands. But that is because we are seeing through the goggles that our paradigm has put on us, where matter and spirit, self and other, masculine and feminine, sex, spirit, art, money, body, power and nature are separate.

But they are all connected. And over the course of the book we will begin to untangle these threads and find ways to reweave them into a new paradigm of power — one that can be shared by both genders, and that does not degrade either those who share in its power, nor the rest of life on Earth.

Power is the outward manifestation of energy.

On a global scale it is recognised that we are entering an energy crisis. The search is on for new sources of energy to replace the dirty, unsustainable and increasingly scarce fuel supplies we have been running on. We are having to move from fossil fuels to renewable sources for our cars and homes. The same is true internally. The energy sources we are running our bodies and culture on are depleting us too. They are dirty and unsustainable. They are killing us and our world. The structures of power are strangling, not supporting, innovation, creativity and community.

Let us call in and create the revolutionary possibility of new sources of energy, and new power structures that the patriarchy denies are feasible or desirable. As Burning Women, we can learn to do this at the most basic level: by consciously working with energy and reweaving the very structure of reality.

Does this sound crazy? Far-fetched? Deluded?

When we talk about energy, it can seem quite abstract and esoteric, but it follows the same patterns and laws as the forms of power we are more familiar with. Electricity is a form of energy — seen in static charge and thunder storms — which we have learned to produce, channel and domesticate only very recently in human history. To our ancestors, electricity would have been akin to magic, and yet in just over a hundred years we have gone from discovering it to basing an entire culture on it.

I believe that in the next hundred years other forms of energy found in nature and our bodies will go through the same process of scientific discovery and harnessing as electricity did in the last century. In a hundred years' time, what I am talking about will not be considered esoteric in any way. But at the moment we only have New Age and non-Western understandings of energy in the body — *chi* from ancient Chinese medicine, *prana* and *kundalini* — the fire of life — from yogic thought, as well as other systems of thought from native cultures around the world.

In terms of our own biological energy, our use of it has been basic, because our understanding and technologies have been basic. We have been in survival mode, just focusing on staying alive, for most of human history. But, as Maslow pointed out, once we have met these needs, our energy can rise to creativity and self-actualisation: we can move beyond surviving into thriving and conscious co-creation. This is where large tracts of the Western population are poised now. We have the possibility, the potential and the obligation to reconfigure how we work, energetically. . . and then we are empowered to rewire and refuel our culture from the inside out. When we do this, we have the power of nature, the secret of the universe, on our side.

We have not been taught how our energy really works, or how to use it. Of course we have not. Those who run the current System do not want empowered individuals who are unwilling to submit to their authority. Because then their game is up. Instead they seek to keep us in a sense of childlike dependence to the patriarchs — both our individual parents, and the state system.

Whilst many people do not mind exchanging their mature power and energy for a parent-figure to care for them, more and more people are saying *no*. The costs are too high.

Burning Woman is she who chooses to step beyond energetic immaturity with her parents and the state, and into her own power, as a creative, healthy, self-sustaining, powerful individual.

This is nothing short of revolutionary.

Patriarchy is neither natural nor inevitable as they tell us. It is man-made. It is acquired mainly unconsciously. And therefore it can be un-acquired and deconstructed — consciously. Not by attack or debate, but through a wholesale divestment of our interests. Once we see how invested we are in it energetically, we realise that we can make conscious choices to take our power out of it: rather like removing our savings from a bank, or changing electricity suppliers. We just need to know how. And when we do it in large enough numbers. . . things will change. Not just in our individual lives, but on a much larger scale. We just need to stop investing in the current system. To stop believing his-stories to be the Truth. To stop being a gullible audience to the illusion of monotheistic patriarchy, and look behind the scenes, at the strings which let them break the laws of nature.

> *The system will collapse if we refuse to buy what they are selling —*
> *their ideas, their version of history, their wars, their weapons, their*
> *notion of inevitability. Remember this: we be many and they be few.*
> *They need us more than we need them. Another world is not only*
> *possible, she is on her way. On a quiet day, I can hear her breathing.*
> **Arundhati Roy**

WHO IS BURNING WOMAN?

This woman burns
Blood red
And orange.
The flames lick her toes, her thighs and up between her legs,
Her womb is consumed, her breasts are on fire,
Her hair alight.
She is gone and in her place ashes and soul.
Burn, woman, burn!
With your own fire and passion.
Burn from the inside,
Out into the world.

Burning Woman is a powerful image. A role model. A metaphor. A warning. She is Feminine power incarnate.

Eve was the first Burning Woman in his-story, punished for her passion with painful childbirth for the rest of his-story. Pandora. Inanna. Cleopatra. The whore of Babylon. The Queen of Sheba. All these are the Burning Women from the ancient pages of patriarchy. Women who loved too much, who were led by their inner voices and sensual bodies to express their passions in their own ways. Each was a woman who dared to wield Feminine power in a patriarchal world. Each was destroyed, and her story passed down as a stark warning to women everywhere of what happens to a woman inflamed by passion. *Beware women*, we were taught, as we listened to their stories, *this is what happens to she who burns too bright. You will fall, and bring curses, punishment and damnation not only upon yourself, but upon all who love and follow you too.*

Our culture has been both wary and obsessed with the woman who burns for millennia. She has always stood as the antithesis to that which the patriarchy holds dear. She is a free-thinker. A questioner of authority. She is multifarious in a world that requires monotheism. She is too passionate, lustful, hungry, too uncontrollable. She is the artist who will enchant you with beauty, the activist who will start a revolution, the harlot who will override your logic, the temptress who will arouse your libido, enflame your emotions, the witch who will cast a spell on you.

Beware!

Beware the woman who burns!

Free-thinking, powerful, passionate women are dangerous to a conservative male-dominated culture. They tend to do what they want and believe is right. . . not what you tell them. And so patriarchal cultures have a deep-seated fear of women in their power, their ability to give life. . . and take life, their uncontrollable emotions, their intuition, their constant changing. Rather than seek partnership with this power, the patriarchal system has chosen to dominate and subdue the women who show signs of it through shaming, branding, naming, ostracising, traumatising, raping, medicating. . . and burning. In patriarchy powerful women are a threat.

Their cautionary tales are intended to cultivate the Good

Girl aspect of ourselves, to shut us down. But when they are heard by the dormant Burning Woman within, they whisper of possibility, their sparks leap out of the pages of history and inflame the hearts of living women. Burning Woman's power is beyond time and place. It is contagious. A woman on fire is a wonderful thing if you are dreaming of a bright new future. A life-sustaining future. Burning Woman is a guiding light, a beacon of hope, a trail-blazer for those of us who dream beyond the strangulation of patriarchy.

Burning Woman does not play by the rules of men. She burns the books of law and reinstates the rule of nature. She refuses to be boxed in. Burning Woman pisses on the patriarchal pyramid, she laughs at the silly hats and fancy names. She calls the women by name, men too. Tells them to come to her in the dark of night and she'll show them what REAL power looks like. Power that makes kings' dicks shrivel up.

Watch out, she calls, *you want to see power? THIS IS POWER!* And unleashes a volcano, a typhoon, an earthquake, a revolution of women. She laughs in uncontrollable glee as they cling to their pyramid in terror, clenching their gold between their butt cheeks.

Burning Woman is she who is inflamed by her own direct connection to the Feminine life force. She who dares to follows her own vision, who speaks up and tells her own stories. She naturally sails counter to what she has been taught. Because what she is taught is how to be a good not-quite-man in a man-made world under a Father God's rules. The process of unlearning is long, as she learns to uncover her own authentic source to life's power, and claims her own authority to navigate her life according to her inner flame, not the outer lights she has been shown.

She has often been depicted in the forms of the dark goddesses: Kali, Medea, Medusa, Oshun and Hecate. When she is given her way, she gives birth to the world. When she is wronged or men try to control her, she destroys with impunity. She is not to be messed with, the embodiment of Feminine power, who dwarfs the masculine and eats the most powerful men as afternoon snacks, adorning her body with their bones.

Our modern cultures fear her destructiveness, and have no place for her and no image of her. Powerful women are not desired by the patriarchy. And so they have painted her out of his-story, taken down her statues, forbidden her worship, silenced her sisters through death and shame. And without her awesome model, without her instruction, women have no archetype to inform them. We have forgotten her knowing.

But we are remembering.

Burning Woman teaches us other ways of power — the fire circle, the spiralling helix of life, the web of interbeing, the multicellular organism — autonomy within interconnected community. She shows us these forms throughout nature. Hers is the power of the pouncing lioness, the roar of a hurricane, the swoop of an eagle, the crashing of a wave, the gentle force of the moon on the tides, the unleashing of a mighty orgasm, the contractions of labour, the spider weaving a web of gossamer silk.

To ally ourselves with her, we must, once again align ourselves with the cycles of the sun, the moon, the planetary movements, the seasons and each other. We can only reclaim our native power, when we realise that we are an integral part of all these things, and they are of us. This power is deeper and stronger than worldly power. It is incoercible, because it is not taken on faith, it is not believed or blindly followed, it is not reliant on the opinions of others: it is known, within every cell of our beings. This power is the life force itself.

LOST ARCHETYPES OF THE FEMININE

Burning Woman is an archetypal figure and one that most women seem to resonate instinctively with: both the inner burning of passion and powerful desires, but also the identification with the terror of being burned, whether shamed in this lifetime. . . or remembering the Burning Times. Despite this universality, I have not come across her discussed anywhere else in terms of archetypes. She is, I believe, a lost archetype of the Feminine, and one who holds the potential key to shifting our relationship to power—inner and outer—in this world.

But what exactly is an archetype, and how do they work?

Archetypes are universal energy patterns which exist in the collective unconscious, emerging with regularity in dreams, art, metaphors and stories. We inhabit many of them over the course of our days, some on occasion, and some as our dominant modes of self-expression. Some of the more commonly-known Feminine archetypes are Queen, Princess, Mother, Virgin, Whore, Heroine other common non-gendered ones include: Teacher, Victim, Martyr, Fool. Over the course of this book we will be meeting: Burning Woman and Burning Man, The Good Girl, The Witch, Starving Woman, The Patriarch, The Shadow Man and The Devouring Mother.

Archetypes have existed in human culture since the dawn of time, but they were brought into modern therapeutic healing work by the founder of analytical psychology, C.G. Jung in the early twentieth century. He believed that the activation or awakening of an archetype releases enormous power within a person. This has certainly been my experience.

We can engage with archetypes in many different ways — through writing, painting, movement, active imagination, story, image work. . . Whether we access them through images or words, or both at once, they provide keys to hidden inner portals of the psyche. The right word, image or phrase can unblock a previous dead end, so that energy can flow once again and our power can be reclaimed.

Archetypes hold fascination for me and I have been researching them informally for nearly twenty years. A large part of my work — in my writing, art and teaching — has been in reclaiming and revisioning lost archetypes of the Feminine.

This was in no small part because I never personally identified with so many of the traditional feminine archetypes — I never aspired to be a Princess (always her father's daughter, never her own woman), never felt as though I were the Good Mother. Even the ancient goddesses and heroines that so many women's books share feel distant and alien to me.

And so in my books I share other archetypes, ones that resonate strongly with women like myself, who inhabit the edges of our culture, the spaces of revolution and foment. They are archetypes for women with powerful energies who do not fit easily into the more passive roles prescribed for us by our masculine culture.

Throughout the book, we will be becoming more familiar with Burning Woman as an archetype and her qualities that we can use as blueprints for our lives. At others, I will be directly addressing you, dear reader, as Burning Woman — to acknowledge these qualities already within you, and help you to embody the archetype further. And occasionally I refer to the Feminine face of God, the divine Feminine, the Goddess, the sacred presence — as the immanent expression of Burning Woman. I trust you will find your way. And the more you immerse yourself in this archetype, the more you will see that these differences are in fact irrelevant. This energy, this consciousness, this power are all the same.

WHAT OF THE BURNING MAN?

Women's liberation has often been portrayed as a movement intent on encroaching upon or taking power and privilege away from men, as though in some zero-sum game, only one gender at a time could be free and powerful. But we are free together. Or slaves together.
Rebecca Solnit, *Men Explain Things to Me*

Many people who read a book of flames which talks of Burning Women, of the patriarchy, often respond: "But what about men? Not all men uphold the values of the patriarchy. What about our gentle sons? Our beloved husbands and caring brothers, our loyal cousins, our treasured creative colleagues and friends? What about them? They suffer too, they struggle too." Yes, they do. They burn too.

Throughout history there have been millions of Burning Men. Men who were burned at the stake. Who burned for the love of a god . . . or a human lover. . . who was not proscribed. Who dreamed of community along different lines. Who healed according to their own authority. Who took up the fight for women, for peoples of colour, for the oppressed, the down-trodden, for wild nature, for crazy dreams and new ideas — who went against the powers-that-be and fought for what they knew to be right. There are millions of men today who heal and vision new paradigms, who paint and write, who protest for rights, advocate for the dispossessed and hold up our culture for the sham it is. Men who stand powerfully beside the women in their lives — who defend the rights and joy of their sisters, wives, mothers and daughters. Men who do not fear the Feminine, but honour it deeply and who are dedicated to embodying the mature Masculine. Men who father from the heart with tenderness. Who make passionate love and lives with their women. Men who live powerfully in partnership.

I have been lucky to have a life full of Burning Men — my

husband, my father, my son, my many male friends, teachers, healers and artists, writers and thinkers who have inspired me. I honour their place in my life deeply. I stand shoulder to shoulder with them. And they with me. We have each other's hearts and backs. We are partners in art, vision, passion, struggle and love as we move into deeper relationship with each other.

There is much we share. We have so much in common.

And we are different too.

This is not about polarisation, or women against men. Nor am I implying obligatory heteronormativity or heterosexuality. We all have both masculine and feminine energetic forces within us and express and relate to them with people of both genders.

Where either gender is in fear of, or feels superior to, the other, there can never be a partnership of equals. This is what we are literally dying for now on Earth: a living partnership of mature Masculine with mature Feminine power. Power with, not power over. A community and culture which respects and encourages autonomy of individual expression — with the proviso that we do not hurt others — without recourse to shame, manipulation, punishment or death.

Burning Woman and Burning Man combine the mature Masculine and Feminine in creative partnership. To get there we have to reclaim the Feminine — women and men both — to travel deep into Feminine power, so that the two can mingle as equals.

THE HERO'S JOURNEY

Aligning our ordinary life with our evolutionary divinity is a path of fire. You burn. You grow. You burn. You grow. Constantly. The only stability is our trust in the process.
Sera Beak, *Red, Hot and Holy*

The quest most of us learn early on is that which is played out in movies and his-story books: the hero's journey. The boy goes out into the world, naïve and innocent, overcomes his weakness and fears, faces trials, slays the dragon to prove himself. In this way he becomes a hero, grabs himself a fair maiden as a reward and so proves himself a man. In this archetypal story lie the seeds of masculine power: public acts of courage, domination and bravado make you top dog and get you a fuck.

Like many of us, I started out on the hero's journey. My dreams from the age of eight would have made Freud proud. Mine was a classic case of penis envy. Night after night I dreamt that my penis had been cut off. This thing of which I was so proud, my source of power, had been sliced at the root. Everyone crowded round to see this penis in a box. It was mine, but it was no longer mine. I felt its loss deeply.

In the waking world I was a high achieving academic from early on, scooping most awards going, top of most classes I was in, passionate about learning and achieving. I lived with my head in a book. I loved Barbies and flower fairies, writing, drawing and dressing up. . . and I also liked Lego, Meccano, rock-climbing in my bare feet and playing football. Blue was my favourite colour. But the older I got, the more I discovered that there were two sets of rules. One for the boys. And another for us girls. And theirs always seemed fairer than ours.

When games of football got too boisterous at break time, the girls were banned. The decree came down from on high: only the older boys could play on the top playground. Everyone else had to share the lower playground. For one of the first times in my life, aged nine and a half, I felt the boiling outrage of a female wronged. I led a delegation of girls up to the headmaster's study to demand our rights. We got them. But this benevolent headmaster's powers only went so far. At eleven I went to the after-school cricket club and played well, but when it came to matches I was categorically not allowed to play. The other schools would not allow a girl in their boys-only club.

Talking of boys-only clubs, I went to church a lot. (I know, you probably weren't expecting that one, were you?) I had a passion for learning more about God. I used to lie in bed at night trying to figure Him out. I loved the music and sang in many choirs. I got top grades in my Religious Studies GCSE and elected to study the Bible as Literature as a module in my first year of University. I went to church twice each Sunday when I was at Cambridge, studying to be a teacher. But as the years went on, I found myself getting angrier and angrier as I sat in church listening to the male priests talking about God our Father. *He. He. He...* until I wanted to scream.

*Why was the omnipotent divine force **male**,* I wondered, *when we're told that God is beyond gender?* And whilst we're on the subject, all creatures were created equal, but Eve got made as an afterthought from a surplus rib? *Please.*

I began to take on the Jehovah's Witnesses who called religiously to our door every Wednesday morning. Each week, I grabbed my Bible and read them tasty titbits of rapes and murders encouraged by this supposedly all-loving God. From this book, the word of God, that was written by men. All men. In which men begat men. And women brought the curse upon our species. I realised in my mid-twenties that I was done with the church as it stood, one that was intolerant of women and gays and didn't practice what JC himself, whom I have down as the archetypal Burning Man, preached.

And as I pulled my power back from those stories, as well as the stories of selling your soul to big corporate cultures for hefty salaries, I began to realise that the hero's journey was not created for me. It was not my story. It held no true reflection of my life, my feelings, my body and its needs. I was trying to prove myself through it, rather than simply be myself.

Throughout secondary and tertiary education, I had driven myself hard externally—I found great satisfaction in achieving.

But in private I was a woman committed to discovering herself on the inside. I had no idea how to share this part of myself, so I hid it away.

I sought out PhD programs abroad which I hoped would lead me towards writing the books I always knew I would write. Lacking a penis for prestige, I felt I needed the authority conferred by the title, Dr, to be able to speak and be heard. I yearned for the masculine stamp of approval, to have the permission to express myself on the public stage and the printed page. But I also knew that by the time I graduated, I would be wanting to have children. My life as I knew it would be over. I was scared of the debt. I was angry that my boyfriend didn't have to worry about these choices and worried that this following of my fire too strongly would burn my relationship up.

So I diverged to playing it safe, stepping away from my doctoral aspirations, instead training to be a secondary school teacher closer to home. I did what so many women do—I chose *acceptable*. I chose *responsible*. I chose *safe*. I played the Good Girl, and folded my book writing dreams up and put them in a dark drawer of my psyche, and instead taught teenagers how to write essays, whilst occasionally taking the authorities to task with revolutionary verve.

But life had other plans. I became pregnant two months into my teacher training course, and started the initiation to motherhood much sooner than expected. With three kids in four and a half years, the urge, the absolute need to reclaim space for myself, to become the 'me' I was outside of motherhood grew stronger and stronger. My embers were burning. I tried to ignore them, but they started scorching my skin. I tried to throw them away. To submerge them in water. To cover them over. It only led to deeper burning. And so I did the only thing I had not done. I leaned towards them and blew, put in my energy and kindled them until they began to grow. I moved from teaching to living. Over the course of eight years a creative writing class I taught in my sitting room turned into my starting to write articles, which turned into a magazine editing job, a column, a blog, then books and a publishing company. It sounds easy, when it is put like that. It was not. Not when my passions are so niche and contradictory. But what I have learned each time, is that the answer lies in uncovering the embers that fuel me, my deepest passion, my strongest fear, my deepest desire—which it is so easy to cover up with busyness and other people's judgements and fear and excuses and the ever-present threat of shame.

I have grown my life's work congruently with my own inner flame. But the shadows it casts, in myself, in others can scare me. I am by nurture conflict averse, needy of other's acceptance and approval — a very strange countenance for someone so at odds with the culture in which she lives. As my work has grown I have found myself separated from my old self. I have two personas which don't seem to meld. The shy, Good Girl me who finds it hard to talk about my work and finds it hard to make conversation at the school gates and who will die if anyone I know reads this book. The one who gets burned by the smallest slight, feeling the acid of words only half meant dig deep into her soul and who dissolves into months of crippling anxiety and depression. And the other me. The me who burns. Burns with revolutionary passion. With a desire to build community, to write and paint, to challenge. These two felt senses of self have been in direct opposition and so I have been trying to find a way to reconcile my Good Girl self, trained as a second-best hero, with my inner Burning Woman on a revolutionary heroine's journey

Having written the paragraphs above, last night I had a dream. I was in a play (drama was my first career path—I gave it up after months of nightmares about opening my mouth on stage and no voice coming out). I was cast as the husband.

We were rehearsing, in front of an audience. My main role was to do the emotions, whilst my wife talked. Then we appeared again at the end of the play. Only this time I was the wife. I worried whether I would I remember all my lines. And then I realised that it would be very confusing to the audience—that I was first the man and then the woman.

I realise on reflection that this has been the way of my life, and that of many women I have spoken to. We start out on the hero's journey—leaving home to find our fortunes, slaying dragons to get glory. The hero's journey is the one our world is based on; girls get the chance to live it too nowadays. As long as they can play the part, and be stronger and cleverer than the men, and can survive the toll it takes on their bodies and spirits.

But then at some point, we realise that we are not men. Living the masculine way, when we are birthing our babies, mothering our children, living in menstrual bodies is profoundly unhealthy for us. Soon we realise that however hard we try to be good men, we are not judged in the same way, paid in the same way, we have to work harder and longer to prove ourselves worthy, and even then we are still not enough. Or maybe our health buckles under the strain of work, marriage or motherhood, the expectation that we care for sick relatives. Suddenly we find ourselves in the dark, sick, depressed, burned out. . .

This is our awakening to the Feminine, if we will take it. It shows us that the hero's journey is not our journey. Ours is the heroine's journey, a spiral journey of inner and outer discovery of our innermost selves and our source of Feminine power. We travel inwards, into dark and unknown terrains, finding our way through to the other side by discovering an inner flame to light our way. As we travel further on we realise that this inner flame is the goal we have been seeking, the guide and ourselves are one and the same, and furthermore the light and the darkness are two parts of the same whole.

We have long inhabited an era of Separation. Separation

of the material from the spiritual, the Masculine from the Feminine, light from dark. And now is the time, when that which has been oppressed is rising to full equality, balancing the imbalance. Now is the time of the maturing of both masculine and feminine, the hero and the heroine, realigning the two powers in their mature expression and partnership.

But before we move forward, first we must spiral back, to see where we have come from and learn from our past experiences and collective conditioning, to examine our fear of Burning Woman as we have been shown her in his-story. We need to understand how the world we inhabit works, understand its power over us, before we can release its spell, and focus on the inner work of rekindling the Burning Woman within.

2
A HISTORY OF BURNING WOMEN

her fire burns hot.
flames lick through me.
but, there's no stake holding me here.
*no, here she burns **for** me,*
the goddess of fire,
to remind me that
deep in my belly a fire should be raging,
burning,
consuming.

. . .

the women of my line,
did they fear this fire?
was fire too close to the history of this line of women immemorial?
I see them, their faces dark,
no firelight in their souls,
no burning in their core,
no fuel to fire longing and desire, to give volume to voice.

this fear of fire,

how deep does it run?

I see them,

a line bleeding back into the dark bowels of centuries past where

no flame burns.

dark faces, tightly drawn skin reminding me of my own jawbone.

how powerful was this message?

put out your light, woman.

by fearing our own fire,

we douse our own flame.

we cannot live what we are here to do without fire.
Julie Daley

In order to fully understand our own limitations, hesitations, blocks and anxieties we have to delve into our his-story. Both the official his-story that we have learned, as well as her-story that has been suppressed. We need to become conscious of the culture that we have numbed to in order to survive. We have to bring into conscious awareness that which goes sensed but unspoken: the threat of being a woman who lives to her own tune in this world.

The next part of this book was hard to write. And may be hard to read. But I believe it is necessary to join up the dots and to feel the emotions that are evoked by the facts: to recognise what we have become blind to, so that we may see more clearly the way ahead.

W IS FOR WITCH

Whenever I hear a guy say, 'She's too wild, too much, too hard to figure out, too complicated, too intense, too hard to handle, too emotional, too opinionated, or crazy.' I hear, 'I'd have burned her ass at the stake back in Salem. She is too connected to the Goddess. I won't be able to tame her.'

Jenny G. Perry

We are the granddaughters of the witches they were never able to burn. If history teaches us that a 'witch' is nothing more than a woman who doesn't know her place, then damn straight, I consider myself a witch.

Ruby Hamad

When I learned my alphabet, W was for witch. The archetypal Burned Woman, there in front of my pre-school eyes. R wasn't for rapist or P for paedophile or psychopath. But there it was: W for witch.

We are taught about the dark feminine early, we imbibe the warning of the witch with our nursery stories. *Beware the solitary woman who lives in the forest, casts spells and will eat human children for breakfast.* And as a perceived pretender to patriarchal power, of course she was depicted in a silly black hat with a phallic broomstick poking out from between her legs.

Want to discredit a woman in the real world? All you need is one word.

Witch.

Still. In the 21st century. Just this week an Australian Federal Minister called a respected political journalist who wrote about a sexism scandal that a senior colleague had just resigned over, "a mad fucking witch".

The W word has been a one-word death sentence to women for centuries. The fire starter. It has been used to condemn women who inhabit the outlying edges of our patriarchal culture and flatly refuse to have their lives decided for them. It has been used to shame and silence those who speak up. As well as those who chose not to marry or have children, who healed using unknown means, who cursed the wielders of power for their inhumanity, who attended deaths and births, or have followed their own spiritual and sexual impulses.

The witch represents the patriarchal fear of women's power, embodied in an individual. She who must be destroyed so that society can prosper. But look a little closer and her spells, her abilities to do the supernatural, to enchant, to shapeshift are, I would argue, paranoid reversals of the equally imaginative claims of the Bible. Her powers are spookily analogous to those assigned to the great heroes of the Bible. But if patriarchs' were done through men, via the power of the male God, then hers, done not in the name of God, must be done in the name of his shadowy counterpart—the Devil.

The witch (AKA a powerful woman) has been pitched as a direct threat to the carefully constructed male dominated system of "divine right". And so the System has done everything within its power to erase, discredit and disconnect women who exhibit any form of power, and label them witches. With society's blessing. Because, throughout history, where women have never been considered as human as men, witches were not human at all. *They do not deserve our pity or defence,* we are told, *we are well rid of them. They would destroy everything we hold dear. And so we must destroy them first.*

We have been told enough fairy stories in our girlhood to know to beware of the witch. We have read enough his-story to know that as women we don't want to be mistaken for her. The desire to live, to be accepted and to belong, keeps most of us in our places. And so we spend our lives running from the darkness, trying our hardest to be good and work hard and keep others happy.

To me, a witch is a woman that is capable of letting her intuition take hold of her actions, that communes with her environment, that isn't afraid of facing challenges.
Paulo Coelho

So when we feel the fire rising in our bellies, we also smell smoke in our nostrils. We feel passion and sense danger. And so we step back, pipe down, play it safe. For fear of what if. Because his-story has taught us clearly: bad girls are branded as witches. Bad girls get burned.

When we feel the upwelling of power within us, our bodies respond with deep fear. Far deeper than just a worry about losing face or looking silly. But rather the threat of losing our lives or those we love. The fear is real. Our bodies know it.

Whether you believe in past lives, in the collective unconscious, the recent scientific discoveries of the cellular transmission of trauma down the generations, or simply in historical awareness, we remember the Burning Times. We remember the high price that was paid for living according to your own inner voice, following your heart, questioning societal norms and being different to your tribe. But don't just take my word for it, this is what a few women have shared with me:

I can't tell you how many times during healing sessions or meditations I have felt the sensation of being burnt. Killed for being who I am, for speaking my truth.
I don't know if this comes from past lives or if it's an ancient echo of human persecution stored in the collective unconscious that I have felt in my own cells. I don't need to know. But each time it's arisen I have felt it as a tangible body experience and each time I have moved through the fear and let it go. This has been part of my healing over the past twenty years — to work with the deep fears that made me feel unsafe to be here, many of them ancient, irrational and deeply ingrained.
Jackie Stewart

When I was doing past life therapy training I had memories often with the sensations of the smoke. I could literally smell the smoke and feel it in my nostrils. Often during physical pain like sinus infections I would have the same memories. We really are stepping away from these centuries of old beliefs.

Marion Rose

Suddenly I dropped to my knees and was transported back to an ancient time, when I was naked, tied to a post with ropes wrapped around my whole torso, dropped to my knees, persecuted as a witch during the Burning Times and left to die, while not only the men but MY SISTERS walked away in fear of their own lives, saying nothing, pretending they didn't know me. Leaving me to die. The ultimate injustice and betrayal. Under the same full moon, I bawled, releasing so much grief for those times of torture, persecution and betrayal, and all the pain, ignorance and suppression that still inflicts our culture to this day. . . and I am SO excited the veils are being lifted now, the pain is being released because it's time for us to RECLAIM our power. And I have no fear now. The witch hunts are over. It's time to come out from the shadows. . .

Avalon

Times are changing.

And yet still we are haunted by the Burning Times of old. They are still alive in us. We must dig deeper.

THE BURNING TIMES

There shall not be found among you any one that makes his son or his daughter to pass through the fire, or that uses divination, or an observer of times, or an enchanter, or a witch.

The Bible, Deuteronomy 18:10

For centuries around the world, the ultimate punishment for women was public death by fire. Perhaps the most well-known

Burned Woman was Joan of Arc who was burned at the stake for her actions and beliefs.

She was not alone. In Europe between 1450-1750 figures ranging from a conservative 35,000 [viii] to a truly terrifying (though discredited by mainstream his-storians) 9 million women were burned as witches. But as Brian A. Pavlac, PhD, Professor of History at Kings College, London, who specialises in the history of the witch hunts reflects, "even the lower figure of under fifty thousand dead would have meant over a hundred thousand put on trial. Then, considering all the personnel involved in the justice system as court officials and witnesses, friends and family members, and those who even felt the 'fear' caused by the hunts, millions of people's lives changed, usually for the worse, because of the witch hunts." [ix]

Whilst the Catholic church started the craze, with the publication of *The Hammer of the Witches,* from 1542 and 1735 a series of Witchcraft Acts were enshrined into law by parliaments around Europe. The punishments — imprisonment, torture and death—were focused on individuals who were deemed to practice witchcraft and magic. [x] Common accusations of witchcraft included: raising storms, giving the evil eye, killing people or livestock or causing bad luck.

To justify the killings both Christianity and secular institutions created ever broader definitions of witchcraft including being "associated with wild Satanic ritual parties in which there was much naked dancing." [xi] Ah, yes, naked dancing. Dangerous stuff that!

And whilst the victims of witch burnings included men and children, Brian A. Pavlac notes that "some witch hunts did almost exclusively target women, in percentages as high as 95% of the victims." Whilst Anne Barstow, author of *Witchcraze* reminds us that the members of the legal system its "judges, ministers, priests, constables, jailers, judges, doctors, prickers, torturers, jurors, executioners" were nearly 100% male.

Radical feminist, Marxist scholar, Silvia Federici, points out in her acclaimed book, *Caliban and the Witch,* that the witch burnings were systematic, happening at the same time as bloody land grabs in Europe and the New World, concurrent with massive increases in the Catholic church and nation states' power and wealth. This domination and brutalisation of nature, native peoples and women was one and the same. It has been argued that witches were burned to coerce women into accepting "a new patriarchal order where women's bodies, their labor, their sexual and reproductive powers were placed under the control of the state and transformed into economic resources." [xii]

Notes Alex Knight in his essay, "Who Were the Witches? — Patriarchal Terror and the Creation of Capitalism": "The witches were those women who in one way or another resisted the establishment of an unjust social order — the mechanical exploitation of capitalism. The witches represented a whole world that Europe's new masters were anxious to destroy: a world with strong female leadership, a world rooted in local communities and knowledge, a world alive with magical possibilities, a world in revolt."

But it wasn't just witches who were burned. In England burning was the most common punishment for women for many other crimes against the patriarchy: plotting to kill the king or any other superior (i.e. male) including her husband. Or for coining (counterfeiting money) which, when you are kept out of the economic system by dint of your gender, would be a reasonably common way to try to gain currency for yourself. [xiii]

It matters. It does. Because those flames that burned our foremothers in their hundreds of thousands burn us still today, albeit metaphorically, for exactly the same reason.

They were burned simply for speaking their own truth. Otherwise known as heresy, "any provocative belief or theory that is strongly at variance with established beliefs or customs."

To be heretical was to be dead.

Look again at that word: Heresy. . . Her say. . .

A woman lived under threat of being burned alive for living, speaking or acting in any way which contradicted or questioned the cultural norms which surrounded her: medical, spiritual or hierarchical. She was burned for earning a living on her own terms. The very systems which told her at every turn that she was a sinner, was less than a man, limited her power, authority, sexuality and economic survival.

Men were burned at the stake it's true, but with far less frequency. The official reason given for the dominance of burning women is that they did not want to expose a woman's body — heaven forbid, we must ensure her modesty even in death — as happened when a person was hung, drawn and quartered. But even the (male) commentators of the time, could see the contradictions: "There is something so inhuman in burning a woman, for what only subjects a man to hanging" (The Times, 1788).

The woman on fire was not a private act. She was burned in public, as a warning to all women: disobey and this will be you.

Women have not been burned at the stake in England since 1790[xiv] and the last trial for witchcraft in the US was as recent as 1833.[xv] But sadly it is not ancient history.

Witch hunts still occur today in societies where belief in magic is prevalent, including sub-Saharan Africa,[xvi] rural north India and Papua New Guinea. According to the World Health Organisation around 500 women a year are killed as witches in Tanzania, and between 2010 and 2012 over 2,100 women were burned as witches in India.[xvii] In Ghana the BBC reported (in 2012) on six witch camps where women who have been accused of witchcraft can flee to safety.[xviii] And in Saudi Arabia (a country with a 57% male population) witchcraft is still legally punished by death.[ix] In 2015 ISIS was reported as having burned two women as witches, and their husbands too, on accusations of "sorcery" and using "magic for medicine". xx

In India the practice of "widow burning" or *sutee* was officially outlawed in 1829, but continued well into the twentieth century. Women who had been widowed would "voluntarily" be burned alive beside their husbands. Though many were bound and forced in order to "show their devotion". This is even more hideous when it is understood that young girls would be married off to much older men. So a girl may be widowed at eleven, having been married for two years, and would then either face a life of shunning and starvation as a "widow" whose sins — in this life, or karma from a previous incarnation —were believed to have brought about the death of her husband. A man's death was always considered the "fault" of his wife.

I want to stop. I want to stop these words and stories, but still they keep tumbling out. I want that writing it will stop this happening. I want to never read or write another list of facts like that again.

But we must learn to see and feel. To feel it fully in our bodies allows us access to the Feminine. We cannot flinch from this reality, from the fear and control and domination of the Feminine by the masculine as it is played out by fathers and husbands and priests and judges in village squares and kitchens and mosques and churches and courts of law around the world.

We must learn to dig down for the very real roots of our fears as they are played out in the world.

We are not crazy.

We are not paranoid.

We are not imagining things.

This is what we fear when we feel our power rising.

This is what we know.

This is real.

HONOUR KILLINGS

The purpose of honour killings is to maintain men's power by denying women basic rights to make autonomous decisions about marriage, divorce and sexuality.
Madre

The right to life for women is conditional on their obeying social norms and traditions.
Hina Jilani

Hear me when I say, this is not just dry history. It is still happening. Women around the world are being burned, simply because they are women.

Acid throwing, breast ironing, bride burning, domestic abuse, female genital mutilation, dowry death, female infanticide, genocidal rape, honour killing, sexual slavery. . . the list of abuses on Wikipedia is there for all to see. Crimes perpetrated on women's bodies. Crimes which have no masculine equivalent.

I feel the bile rising, the acid in my throat.

The rise of acid attacks around the world is a newer form of burning. This is a relatively new way of destroying a woman's highest currency within patriarchy: her beauty and sexual desirability, as revenge for perceived disloyalty. The belief being, if *that* man can't have her, then *no one* will. He will brand her for her wrongdoing and mark her for life in the eyes of the world, melting her identity and female self, imposing his passion and rights on her body.

As Rebecca Solnit notes, "Violence is one way to silence people, to deny their voice and their credibility, to assert your right to control over their right to exist."

Especially when those people are physically smaller, economically and socially weaker than you. . . and you have the law on your side.

In India, Pakistan and the Middle East — home to over two billion people — women suspected of adultery, who seek divorce, are raped, or refuse to marry the partner chosen for them by their families can be burned alive by their families in "honour" killings. According to the UN over 5,000 women a year die this way. At the hands of their family members. In the name of honour.

Honour killings use violence and fear as tools of control. In many cultures where honour is a person's greatest social asset, men are seen as sources or agents of that honour, whereas the only effect that women can have on honour is to destroy it. Once the honour is destroyed by the woman, there is a need for immediate revenge to restore it, in order for the family to avoid losing face in the community. The murders are often performed in public to warn the other women within the community of possible consequences of engaging in "illicit behaviour".

The human rights body, Amnesty International, notes:

The regime of honour is unforgiving: women on whom suspicion has fallen are not given an opportunity to defend themselves, and family members have no socially acceptable alternative but to remove the stain on their honour by attacking the woman.

In India and Pakistan there is also the culture of bride-burning, when a young woman is murdered by her husband or his family for her family's refusal to pay an additional dowry. The woman is typically doused with kerosene and set alight. This practice is relatively recent and has been particularly virulent since the 1980s. Over 2500 women a year die this way.

Whilst the Western world no longer burns women physically, we still have a culture viciously intent on shaming and destroying the livelihoods, reputations, bodies and mental health of women who challenge the status quo. And we still use the term "witch hunt" to describe this act of seeking and persecuting any perceived enemy, particularly when the search is conducted using extreme measures and with little regard to actual guilt or innocence. Still we "burn" those who step too far out of line: see the shocking treatment of home birth midwives, feminists and female activists who are treated disproportionately in comparison to male counterparts.

And women still die violently today — three women daily in the US — at the hands of partners, or ex-partners. Three. A day.

In all these cases, honour is defined by the patriarchy. And judged by the patriarchy. And women pay the ultimate price.

Why?

I'll tell you why.

WOMAN AS SINNER

The word 'sin' is derived from the Indo-European root 'es' meaning 'to be.' When I discovered this etymology, I intuitively understood that for a [person] trapped in patriarchy, which is the religion of the entire planet, 'to be' in the fullest sense is 'to sin'.

Mary Daly, *Gyn/Ecology*

They said I destroyed the world with my sin — it was my fault. My wickedness was to blame — and Jesus, a man, had to suffer a terrible death to make it right. I, a woman, and all the other women like me, carried the burden for everything that was not right with the world. And I believed them. I did not disagree. At the trials, when they accused me, said what I did was evil — I could not remember, was I? I became confused. They said I was unclean, that their god regarded us as filth, that our kind had brought pain to the world. I was guilty. After a while, I couldn't remember — perhaps I was. I now remember, my confusion clears, the veils are lifting. I remember my innocence. I lift the burden from my shoulders, and from other women's shoulders. I again walk proud and free.

Glenys Livingstone, *PaGaian Cosmology*

Because we're women. And women are bad. That's what most major cultures and religions have taught.

Women as harlots and sinners, as temptresses and wicked mothers litter the pages of the sacred texts and children's fairy tales alike. Women deserve to suffer and die.

As we have seen in this chapter, to be a woman is to be a constant actor in a moral universe created and judged by men. Your best way of surviving it is to be good.

To be a Good Woman is to constantly work to atone for your inherent unworthiness. To sacrifice yourself, your time, your vision, your dreams in the service of others. To be a Good Woman is to uncomplainingly do the work of others and never say "no". To be a Good Woman is to tame yourself, to shave your body hair, curl your eyelashes, paint your face and hide your soul in a quiet corner. The Good Woman, the ideal woman is domesticated, beautiful to look at, doesn't take up too much space, is quiet, obedient, hard-working, God-fearing and dispensable. A Good Woman is submissive and compliant —always sexually available, but only to her assigned partner.

In a universe where the rules are always set externally and can change at a whim, a woman must always be on her guard. She is expendable, so she has to work extra hard to keep favour. A woman is never enough as she is. She has no intrinsic value but exists only in relationship to her usefulness to others, mainly to create and sustain life.

The best sort of woman, patriarchy tells us, is the silent, invisible woman. The woman shrouded in a veil, the woman hidden away at home, the uncomplaining mother pulling the double shift, the smiling assistant. Society has been intent on erasing women from the arts and sciences, from healing and spiritual practice, from positions of public power, political influence or independent wealth. Her entire identity was, over the course of several hundred years, legally erased until she became merely her father's chattel to be handed on to her husband. A married woman at the turn of the twentieth century had no identity in law: her possessions, her children, her name were her husband's. She was not a being in her own right. This is what our grandmothers experienced. This is what we are recovering from: a total annihilation of being.

Many conservative patriarchal traditions from Christian to Muslim in the twenty-first century still worship at the altar of the invisible woman. And those of us that are not controlled by such strictures have still learned to erase ourselves through dieting, and not speaking up for ourselves, using quiet voices, and apologising for ourselves. In the wise words of Rebecca Solnit:

> *Some women get erased a little at a time, some all at once. Some reappear. Every woman who appears wrestles with the forces that would have her disappear. She struggles with the forces that would tell her story for her, or write her out of the story [. . .] The ability to tell your own story, in words or images, is already a victory, already a revolt.*

But it is not just our bodies we are taught to hide, we are also warned of the darkness inside, which, we are told, women have more of: moodiness, anger, depression, resentment, lust, jealousy. Deny them, we are taught early on, resist them, leave them in the dark, inside of you. These are sins, the devil's work, signs of mental illness. Never let them see the light of day, we are warned —do not speak of them and certainly don't express them. Lock them up in your own personal Pandora's box within, throw away the key. Never even admit to its existence. Death to the Dark Feminine. Erase your basic instincts.

The rules are clear: if you will not be a Good Woman, if you will not be silent or sacrifice yourself, quietly happy, if you will not domesticate yourself fully, comply unquestioningly, or work double time, you will be sacrificed on the altar of patriarchy. You will be burned.

And you will deserve it.

WOMEN ON THEIR BACKS

Passionate, free-thinking women have never been appreciated by the religions of the world. Because passionate free-thinking women raise passionate, free-thinking children who grow up to be passionate, free-thinking adults, who are very difficult to manipulate, and almost impossible to control.
Marianne Williamson,
address to the 2015 World Parliament of Religions

Almost every major culture in the past 2,000 years or more has sought to control women's power, by controlling their bodies and energy — sexual, creative and spiritual. They have limited and controlled women's sexual expression, where and how they give birth, how they display their bodies in public and private. Women have become a finely choreographed performance, directed by male stage directions, for the purpose of the male gaze.

For centuries women have been kept on their backs by the system: the most vulnerable, least empowering place to be. We have been forced into birthing on our backs in hospital beds and making love in the missionary position. One in five will be raped or sexually abused in our lifetimes.

The result of this? The World Health Organisation is clear:

Depression, anxiety, psychological distress, sexual violence, domestic violence and escalating rates of substance use affect women to a greater extent than men across different countries and different settings. Pressures created by their multiple roles, gender discrimination and associated factors of poverty, hunger, malnutrition, overwork, domestic violence and sexual abuse, combine to account for women's poor mental health. There is a positive relationship between the frequency and severity of such social factors and the frequency and severity of mental health problems in women. Severe life events that cause a sense of loss, inferiority, humiliation or entrapment. [xxi]

In healthcare, love making and childbirth — three of the most potentially transformative and empowering processes of a woman's life, the "woman on her back" model has brought pain, trauma, fear and systematically removed a woman's sense of control over her own body. It has actively blocked or removed pleasurable hormonal feedback loops, which are her biological markers for optimal health and power. Pain overtook pleasure as a woman's default body state. Trauma has become standard.

None of these "woman on her back" practices are natural to us: they are literally man-made. The missionary position was introduced as a "more civilised" and "godly" form of procreation to tribal peoples around the globe as part of Christian missionaries' duty to rid "baser" peoples of their more "animalistic" practices. Missionary position sex was advocated by Victorian mothers to their daughters with the recommendation that they "lie back and think of England." Hardly a ringing endorsement of pleasure or passion. Sexual numbing had begun, one which was continued through the practice of mainstream pornography, as women learned to perform sex in the male gaze, rather than to feel it.

The lithotomy position or birthing on the back is not practiced by indigenous peoples who prefer upright birthing positions on all fours or squatting, which engage the mother's muscles and use gravity to aid delivery. Nor is it recommended today by the World Health Organisation, who note that it only improves working practice for physician, rather than the birthing experience of the mother. Or the birth outcome. The position was introduced by Louis XIV so that he could observe his mistress in labour as an erotic thing (note, the male gaze), and caught on as a fashionable way to give birth. As male doctors (who did not know what labour felt or looked like — and more male gaze) took over from female midwives, they increased their involvement in the birthing process. Birthing women moved from actively birthing their babies, to being patients. This became the norm, under the guise of progress, spurred on by shaming and scaremongering those who would not comply. There became a growing focus on numbing the woman through anaesthesia. Greater interventions were carried out —or required —which left the women further traumatised —physically and emotionally—and further disempowered.

And so, whether in sex or birth or medicine, the numb, patient, supine woman with her legs splayed under masculine gaze became the norm. She was not the active subject of her own life but a (traumatised, dominated) object acted upon by the masculine.

Think for a moment of a beetle —turn it over onto its back and it is helpless. The same goes for most animals —chickens, pigeons, guinea pigs—turn them onto their backs and they are defenceless, their soft bellies and vital organs exposed.

Peter Levine writes compellingly in his ground-breaking book on healing trauma, *In An Unspoken Voice,* about experiments where animals were turned onto their backs, and not held down. If they were caught calmly and were not fearful, they would pause for a second or two and then flip themselves back over and run off. If they were stressed or fearful when they were caught, they would either attack, or would remain prostrated on their backs for several minutes, or even a couple of hours, despite not being restrained in any way, before getting back up. This is known as *tonic immobility.* It is a natural instinctive behaviour, which kicks in in some positive circumstances — such as a kitten being carried by the scruff of its neck by its mother, or in humans after orgasm. But it is also activated in times of trauma, a sort of systemic playing dead, which we see in rape victims or prey being caught by a predator.

This pattern of putting women on their backs, the embodied trauma which we now know is passed on—both genetically and through upbringing — all have compounded the submission and systemic disempowerment of women. Women have been turned into living dolls: submissive, infantilised, hard-working, uncomplaining, baby-making and minding playthings for men.

If you scare a woman about some of the peak power experiences of her life, the places where she touches her power —menstruation, sex and birth, healing from illness—and if you do this consistently, before, during and after, you can bypass her innate power. Add in the dynamic of practitioners—doctors or husbands—who are in a higher social position, possessed of greater physical strength, and holders of unimpeachable cultural power. For good measure, teach a woman to be ashamed of the powerful parts of her body—her vulva, vagina, womb, breasts and brain—to the extent that she cognitively disengages from them and cannot speak about them, then you hold her power. She will not, cannot, oppose you. She is energetically castrated. She will not burn you down.

This is how trauma has been used as an act of war against the Feminine through the bodies of women.

And it works.

In her constant numbing and shutting down to her body, a woman has to experience greater levels of pain before she will respond. So, for example, during birth, if you also remove from her the coping mechanisms of pain—movement and sound, safety and a known, trusted attendant—then her senses are wide open and her neural pathways are burned with powerful memories. Her body stores the trauma in her cells and activates genes responsible for anxiety in her baby, as has been shown by recent studies in epigenetics. [xxii] Furthermore, trauma in birth commonly triggers attachment issues between mother and baby, and post-natal anxiety and depression in the mother. Trauma upon trauma, generation upon generation all the way down the Motherline.

But then, when the ordeal is over, you force more cognitive dissonance by insisting that her experience is of no importance, everything is okay. Her feelings and experience are both negated and denied, and her physical pain dismissed. She is encouraged to be strong and hold her counsel by all the fellow traumatised women who have been through the process before her — her membership of the sisterhood requires her silence. Her initiation is complete.

This is the submission of women. This is its complexity. The many-edged sword of tribal shaming, biological trauma and systemic disempowerment, reinforced by morals, a hierarchical system and cognitive dissonance, inherited genetically and through upbringing for multiple generations, with plenty of systemic abuse and supernatural threats thrown in for good measure, plus economic and social sanctions and the ever-present threat of death or incarceration for those who do not comply.

No wonder women are scared. No wonder women's empowerment is such a big deal. No wonder it is so complex.

But we have not finished. It goes deeper still.

STARVING WOMAN

As women we have been taught to fear our hunger.

We have learned to fight it, to diminish it and to be disgusted by it.

Our hunger is real and will not be denied, no matter how much we compromise, settle, shrink or try to hide it.

Our hunger is holy.

May we see our hunger in the light of truth, for what it really means.

It means we are alive—alive in the face of enormous obstacles and challenges.

It means that we are hungry for larger visions and expressions of

ourselves and our potential. . .
The only thing that will ever satisfy and fill this hunger.
The hunger to occupy every cell fully and completely,
To abide unapologetically in every nook and cranny of your
complex and brilliant self. . .
This hunger may bring with it an ancient anger.
This anger comes from the frustration of being separated from
ourselves—starving for ourselves!
Generations upon generations of hungry women, ravenous for
what is real and true in ourselves and in the world.
Feel into the legitimacy of this hunger. Own this hunger.
Because only in owning it can it ever be really satisfied.
Anger will eventually give way to a fierce clarity—
A clarity of what must be done to access and live from the inner
nourishment.
Let nothing stand between you and your overflowing banquet,
your inner abundance of Being.
Give guilt no place at the table of your Self.
You are all yours.
Every last morsel.
Bethany Webster

The starvation of women, enforced feminine emptiness, has been the endgame of the System around the world, for generations. Food, the basic energy source of life, has been used to communicate women's inferior power status. And then in a last insult, our hunger has been twisted into some spiritual high for the personal and, even greater, good.

Around the world women eat separately. Differently. In many cultures they eat after the men, and the children, often in a different room. [xxiii] Or they eat vegetables where the rest of the table has meat. In Western countries they survive on salad and smoothies, pass on dessert and pinch their thighs in disgust. Or they eat junk on the go. . . whilst packing nutritious lunches for their families.

It starts young. Women have been found to breastfeed their girl babies for a shorter time than their boy children. [xxiv] In developing countries throughout Asia and Africa studies show that by the age of five considerably more girls than boys are malnourished. [xxv] In America half of three- to six-year-old girls worry about becoming fat. 81% of ten-year-old girls have admitted to dieting. In the words of Catherine Bertini, Executive Director of the World Food Programme, "Women eat last and eat least." [xxvi]

We start our lives hungering for more than we are given, and find it hard to accept that we deserve less, just because of our female anatomy. But we are taught it time and again: as women we are less than, our needs are surplus to requirement.

Until, eventually, we swallow this lie down as truth.

Women's hunger is political. We have not just been starved of energy from physical sustenance, but kept from the table in all ways — from boardrooms to men's clubs to swanky business dinners — these are the places that the deals that are made and circles of power cemented. We have cooked the food, and served the food, arranged the flowers and washed the plates. But we have not sat down to the table as equals.

Most women are hungry: whether it be for food, for equality, to be seen, to be heard, to express themselves, to be acceptable, to be enough. These needs are what smoulder in the guts of every Burning Woman, just waiting to be fed with enough oxygen to take flame.

The breath of life must come from deep within.

But instead of breathing deep into our bellies, we are told to hold them in. Our waists have been constricted by centuries of fashion from corsets to skinny jeans. We have been taught to turn the tools of oppression upon ourselves, our sisters and daughters. We have been taught to starve ourselves, deny our appetites, restrain ourselves in public, to make ourselves smaller. We have learned to circumvent our hungers in all sorts of creative ways: exercising obsessively; bingeing in the darkness; taking appetite suppressants; snatching and grabbing what we desire shamefully in private; stuffing ourselves to satiation and beyond into bloating and discomfort. We do it with food, and we do it with commitments that we take on. We are never in charge of our own enough. We are not allowed, we do not allow ourselves, breathing space.

Hunger is the enemy with which most women are engaged in a Cold War for most of their adult lives. 65% of the female US population between the ages of 25 and 45 report disordered eating, with a further 10%, displaying symptoms of full-blown anorexia or bulimia. [xxvii] Of the 30 million people diagnosed with eating disorders in the US, 90% of them are female, [xxviii] yet only one in ten receive treatment. [xxix] 91% of female college students have attempted to control their weight through dieting. [xxx] 25% of them engage in bingeing and purging as a weight-management technique. [xxxi]

So often it is marked down as a women's problem: weak, flawed, vain, unstable women. Rather than the political issue it is. We have been taught that we are too much: too loud, too needy, too emotional, that we take up too much space for what we are worth. And so we are silently shamed into smallness. Our concerns are trivialised. Our relationship with our own right to exist is deeply conflicted. We are always in some form of apology for our flawed existence.

I believe in the power of the body. And so does the patriarchy. It's why they've shamed our female bodies so long. A woman's body has not been her own. It has been dictated and controlled by governments, families and religions. It's why in so many cultures around the world, throughout history, women have been shrouded in shame—full body clothing, veils and covered hair. Where a man can go bare-chested on the street, a woman doing so is committing a criminal offence. Breastfeeding is hidden away in toilets or under shawls. Abortion is controlled by male law makers and religious leaders. Menstruation is depicted with blue "blood" in TV ads. And whilst penises are doodled everywhere and joked about on day time TV, a woman's genitals are invisible in our culture—from graffiti to art—they are the ultimate taboo. Except in porn. Which has become increasingly violent.

Control and punishment of the female body is the most defining factor of patriarchy. And as the women's movement to power rose in the Western world, and women began to take up more space in public, it is no coincidence that new forms of impossible physical perfection were demanded of them, in order to reinstate control. Naomi Wolf was right on the money when she observed in *The Beauty Myth* that, "Dieting is the most potent political sedative in women's history; a quietly mad population is a tractable one."

Diets and body shame are distractions — distractions from our power, our creativity, our unique beauty, our ability to make a difference in our own lives and in the world. If we are focusing on the size of our butts, or our blocked pores, we are not focusing on inequality outside of us. If we are focused on surviving our own self-imposed starvation, we are not able to focus on our other hungers.

We have been starving for too long.

And it's worked to keep us out of our power.

Until now.

Change is coming, we can smell it, we are ravenous for it,

Like anyone who has been starved

For a few thousand years.

SEEING RED

We see red, not as a mist but clear and scarlet. Cherish it, for this is how the future will be made.
Suzanne Moore

*I was taught as a girl
in a patriarchal household that rage was not an
appropriate feminine feeling, that it should be not
only not be expressed but be eradicated.*
bell hooks

How are you feeling? Are you angry yet? Seeing red? Enflamed? Fuming? If so, good! Really feel that fire in your belly and let it simmer.

As women we get so numb to the System, we shrug our shoulders at the sheer scale of it. Even the thought of it makes us feel powerless. We try to shut it out. *It's too big*, we tell ourselves, *there's nothing I can do.* And so we choose to live in our own relatively safe little bubbles of daily life. Or we try to convince ourselves that it's not so bad, or it's happening elsewhere, to someone else. It's not our problem. We turn off the news and try to carry on, ignoring the little twinges as we read of another rape or traumatic birth or beaten woman or honour killing or the kidnapping of four hundred African schoolgirls or another girl losing her life to an eating disorder.

Nice girls don't feel angry. We are taught that early on. We should focus on the positive. Send love and light.

And so we push it down, distract ourselves, and learn to turn the anger in on ourselves, to pick ourselves apart. And gradually we become fragmented in order to survive, cutting off from our bad body parts, our big feelings, our traumatic memories, the horrific news stories.

And rather than get mad, we get sad. It's easier to cry quietly under the covers than yell in someone's face. We have been socialised to express anger as sadness. It's the safety valve for when it all gets too much. Or we turn the anger in on ourselves. It makes us sick. Makes us bitter.

Bitter women express their anger the only way they are allowed — in nagging, complaining, group bitching, passive aggression and with side swipes of shadow power. Women who aren't allowed to be angry wolf down tubs of ice cream that they don't want. Or starve themselves, or dye their hair, or go on shopping sprees. Or they get angry with the wrong people about the wrong things.

What women tend not to do is take their anger to the man. Or rather to the System. Because the System is faceless and irreproachable. We dare not say what we really feel: *HOW DARE YOU!* For fear of what will happen. And so we stew in our own juices, making ourselves and those around us crazy instead. We swallow our anger down so often, justify reality so frequently, that we become numb to it all.

In the System, the masculine has the stranglehold on anger. The divine right to rain wrath down on the heads of those who displease him. *Wait till your father comes home, and he'll set you right,* we are warned as children, or *God will punish you.*

An angry man is a valid reflection of a righteous Father God and his aggression is seen as a natural part of a testosterone driven male. The feminine, however, is supposed to be pure in her devotion and gentle in her manner, like the Virgin Mary, the ultimate Good Girl. The angry woman is seen as an anomaly, totally possessed by her rage. She is literally mad, the crazy woman. . . and in times gone past would have been locked up in the mad house for an outburst at authority.

Only bad women get angry. Bad women, like. . . I don't know. . . feminists. Interestingly enough the most common way of defining feminists is angry. In the fine tradition of Burning Women, feminists have been described as bra burners, though, as Mary Daly points out, the actual cases of women burning bras were few and far between.

It's all rather depressing isn't it?

Ah, but that's how we've responded, as women, by getting depressed, rather than angry. Depression in adult women is twice as common as in men. [xxxii] Depression has its roots in profound hopelessness and systemic exhaustion. No wonder women struggle so much with it. Depression is a turning inwards of anger and despair on the self, rather than the outward focus of anger.

But anger is the key. As Mary Daly so ably says: "Unlike depression, which is a defeated withdrawal and turning one's energy against the Self, righteous anger is expression of creativity and hope." Burning up injustice in white hot words and furious emotion. Anger is explosive and raw and real. Anger hurts. . . but it can also heal.

Anger is like water: the shape it takes comes from the container you put it in.
Leymah Gbowee, Nobel Peace Prize winner

Anger is the opposite energetic pole of obedience, passivity, submission. Anger shows your inner fire is still burning when someone else tries to define you, to take your power away and destroy what you love.

The feeling of anger can be scary. Burning through logic and love until we are raw, bare and trembling. Anger is a primal emotion — it comes from the reptilian, primitive brain — the part of the brain that does not work with logic. This is why we have to express it in other ways — through yelling, screaming, hitting and in less destructive ways painting, movement and sound.

Now it's all very well talking about anger, but I, like so many women, hate confrontation. Having grown up around intermittent fire storms between my feuding divorced parents,

I learned to run and hide at the sound of a raised voice. Where my father thrives on it — the name of his autobiography was *Warrior Spirit!*—I will do anything to avoid it.

I remember a conversation with him when I was twenty in a Japanese restaurant in London. He was reading *Anger* by the Buddhist monk, Thich Nhat Hanh and recommended it to me and my then-boyfriend. I said I didn't get angry. Just sad. And so didn't feel able to take part in the conversation which ensued between these two men I loved. That moment has stuck with me throughout the years.

How come I don't get angry? I wondered. And then I realised: *I do.* I am angry most of the time. It is my default setting. But it is a silent, fuming inner anger, an unexpressed shaking of my fists at the world. I am terrified of expressing it. I have tried it a couple of times and it was met with fury I found unbearable. At times it erupts in a deluge of words and tears to friends or my husband when it builds up too high. Fire storms of pre-menstrual rage. But not expressing anger at those who anger me.

Bestselling parenting author, Steve Biddulph, raised an interesting point in a recent column in Juno magazine, about how boys learn to turn sadness into anger from a young age. He noted how they then go out into the world destructive and emotionally disconnected. . . but powerful. Women, I realised, on reflection, do the opposite, turning anger into sadness. We learn to turn the potential power of anger and the ability to protect oneself emotionally into excessive emotionality. We are socialised from a young age out of our anger, out of our power. . . and into tears and powerless victimhood.

Just imagine for a moment what would happen if women, individually, united, got angry about the injustices they face. Imagine if we focused our power. The walls of civilisation as we know it would come tumbling down pretty fast. This is already happening in the groups of mothers in Argentina who demand to know the whereabouts of their "disappeared" loved ones; the vigilante gangs of women in India who give vicious reprisals to men known of raping or beating women in their communities; Malala Yousafzai risking death to campaign for girls' rights to education; brave women speaking out about female genital mutilation leading to its criminalisation in many countries; birth activists — including myself — campaigning for the right to birth at home; the young women of Femen who bare their breasts in public and protest at social injustice.

Dare you feel your anger? Dare you express it?

Anger says enough.

This stops here.

The sparks light the pyre

Come dance round the fire!

BURNING THE RULEBOOK

Down with the Fatherland!

Here rises a brave new world,

Shimmering in possibility.

Alive with feeling.

My ticket there is to

Burn the complications

Burn the need to please

Down on my knees

I long to be free

To be me.

Burn my high heeled shoes, my his-tories

My bra, with ease,

Naked and free

I stand on my own two feet.

Free.

From my obligations

And your assignations

The control of nations. . .

This is my body.

On fire with my life

Two feet planted

Under the flag of me

Breasts jutting

Hips strutting

Eyes shutting

The mystery void

The Universe's wondrous vagina

Opens for me

And births me out free.

We live in the context of patriarchy, by patriarchal rules, in patriarchal reality. We know nothing else. We are offered no alternatives, no other frame of reference. It is the air we breathe. We are so used to living in a foreign land and feeling like strangers trying to talk in a language that is not our mother tongue. But because this is all we have known, since birth, we are used to always feeling at odds, divided from ourselves, fragmented, crazy or just plain wrong. We have been taught to keep silent every time we feel this divergence; we have learned to second-guess our instinctive responses. We have learned not to trust our feelings. And so we become avid rule followers, or rebels. Either way, it is the rules, our adherence or rebellion to them, that dictate our lives.

I long to declare an end to playing by the rules (says the woman who is just about to assiduously file her tax return!) Oh, I see the irony. The Good Girl inciting rebellion from her armchair.

I get so bored of rules, so tired of being the Good Girl, for fear of *what if*. More and more of our lives seem wound round and round by red tape, it wraps me so tight I can hardly breathe. Everywhere I look the walls are closing in on my freedom, the noose is getting tighter and tighter as they demand more money, more perfectly filled out forms, more obedience. I want to scream.

I want revolution but I don't want to go to war with the warrior. I have no desire for more hatred and hurt, more fear or trauma. I am sick and tired of this. I have been making myself safe to appease daddy, God our Father, Big Brother and keep him on side, something, anything to live in peace. But it's not working. The more we stay silent, the more power they grab, the more laws they write limiting our power.

How can we change the system and free ourselves from its shackles without perpetuating the cycle of violence? How can we burn the old life-denying culture without loss of what we treasure?

Revolutions in the masculine sphere tend to be enacted by force from without. How can we create an internal revolution? How can we burn the rulebooks in our own lives, so that we can become inflamed with life herself and then unleash THAT power out in the world? What would happen if we stepped into the fire? Not one by one, but *en masse*? What would happen if we unleashed our collective roar on the world?

Feel it rise, your burning passion, your anger, your fury, your hunger for more and different.

I am feeling it to. You are not alone. Dare we commit to it and stand our ground in the swirl of these feelings?

There, in the midst of it all, is your roar. Your Feminine power which will spark your fire. This is your sacred truth that you were born into the world to share. It is time to step into it. To unite your passion with action. To express your deepest self. To come fully alive.

Watch the smoke rise as the dead wood of his-story goes up in the flames of Burning Women around the world. Let us find the courage to join them. Let the undergrowth burst into flame until the skies darken with the shame of the aggression towards the Feminine throughout his-story. Let the fire heal and purify the old. Let it create fertile ground for the new.

We are leaving this reality behind, stepping out of the man-made world, walking beyond his-tory and into our own stories. Telling them in our own words, painting them in our own images.

As the smoke from the bonfires of the past engulf us and darkness overcomes our senses, let us turn our vision inwards to find the new sparks of life which will power this new world.

In order to find the Burning Woman within, we must keep moving into the darkness. We must learn to work in the dark, in order to find the source of the fire.

Take courage and follow me, sister. Into the darkness.

BURNING QUESTIONS ⅋ FIRESTARTERS

At the end of every section there are burning questions and firestarter exercises to help integrate what you have read into your body and soul. These should start sparks in you and help deeper reflection in your creative, spiritual practice and growth. They are listed by section for ease of reference. The intention is to create an immersive, multi-sensory somatic experience, much as the writing of this book has been for me.

So grab your journal and a pen, or your computer. . . meditate on these questions. . . paint or dance your responses. . . bring your answers into the world through your life.

FIRE AND THE FEMININE

What does the Feminine mean to you?

What does it look like?

Who or what represents it for you?

How is your definition similar or different to mine? What have I said that has changed—or clarified—your own understanding?

What has your relationship to the Feminine been over the course of your life?

How and why has it changed? What helped you to form your views?

How does the Feminine relate to the Masculine for you? Ideologically and in your own lived experience?

BURNING WOMAN

Have you come across Burning Woman before? If so, where?

What resonance does she have for you? What mystery does she hold?

What do you burn for? How have you been burned?

What has your image of women and the Feminine been up to now? Watery? Fiery?

Where are you frozen?

Where are you silenced and do not dare to speak?

What Burning Women do you have in your life? Authors, teachers, friends. . .

What do they stand for?

How might you add your voice to theirs?

How can you build your community of Burning Women?

Firestarter

Create an image of the archetype of Burning Woman. What does she look like? What symbols represent her? Paint her, draw her, collage or art journal her. Sculpt her from clay or papier maché, needle-felt or knit her. . . what colour and form suits her best? Where might you keep her so her presence is visible to you as you read?

BURNING MAN

What has your experience been of Burning Man?

What Burning Men do you have in your life? Authors, teachers, friends. . .

How can you build your community of them? How do you work in partnership with them?

How do Burning Women and Burning Men interact?

THE W WORD

What is your relationship to the word *witch*? How much power does it hold for you?

Have you had any experiences of the Burning Times? Dreams, memories, visions? What did you learn about them in school?

Has this section awoken anything in you?

Firestarter

Listen to this Christy Moore song, *The Burning Times*, https://youtu.be/RntnpYTfpSc and allow your body to move to it if you feel it, allow yourself to sing along. . . and afterwards write or draw or paint what comes up for you.

STARVING WOMAN

What is your currently relationship with your body like?

In what ways have you been starved, and how do you starve yourself?

What do you believe you gain by starving yourself? How do you compensate for your starvation?

What are you hungry for? Have you ever considered your hunger as holy?

How long have you been denying or ignoring your hunger?

What do you believe will happen if you allow yourself to have what you desire?

Firestarter

Body photography or art projects on the subject of your body are powerful transformative tools. Possibilities include:

› Self-portraits of your face in a variety of styles and media.

› Self-portraits of your whole body.

› An intimate self portrait of your yoni.

› Taking a photograph each day which truly reflects your inner world.

› Writing a love letter to your body.

› Five Rhythms dance.

› Sculpting your body in clay.

ANGER

What are you angry at right now? Write out a whole list — new angers, old angers, everything that is churning in your body. Dare to give them voice and see what happens.

Where in your body do you feel them?

What does your body and inner self believe will happen if you express your anger? Has this ever happened? If so, how did you respond?

What do you do with your anger?

Firestarter

Feel your anger. Dare to write it out. Shout it out. Paint it out... feel its force and express it. Not necessarily *at* anyone. Just let it out. Don't channel it at me! Don't channel it at yourself. Follow its river of fire. Where does it lead you? What new terrain does it take you to, however crazy and "illogical" it may seem? Remember that branding our deep intuition as illogical is the first way of be-witching women and making them "crazy". Let it tell you what it needs to.

BURNING THE RULEBOOK

Firestarter

Write out a list of rules that you currently follow — consciously or unconsciously. Consider as you write them out: who set these rules and when? What are the penalties for breaking them... according to whom? Have you ever experienced punishment for breaking them? What did this teach you?

Create a burning ceremony. Burn this rulebook.

Now, write your own... based on your values.

3

THE MASCULINE DARK

We all need to look into the dark side of our nature, that is where the energy is, the passion. People are afraid of that because it holds the pieces of us that we're busy denying.

La Gitana Eva

Tell me, sister, are you scared of the dark?

For generations women have been taught to be afraid of the dark. We have been raised to follow the rules, to stay in well-lit areas, for fear of what may befall us in the dark. *Stay in the light*, we are warned, *stay safe, stay home*. In the masculine dark, men are heroes. . . and women are prey.

We know the story of the dark. Or at least the masculine dark.

In the masculine paradigm, the dark is the home of Death, a lone male figure, hooded darkness personified and armed with a blade, menacing and arbitrary in his culling. We spend our lives fleeing from Death, avoiding its path, making deals with it, inviting it prematurely, calling its bluff.

In the Abrahamic religions darkness is equated with the absence of God.

In the beginning all was darkness, so the story goes. *Then God made the light and the darkness was banished.* So begins the founding tale that many of us grew up with within the religions of our fathers. And ever since then they have been saying, *let there be light*.

And so began the battle between good and evil, dark and light, masculine and feminine, the battle between two superpowers which has engrossed humanity ever since.

In the patriarchal system, black and white have been portrayed as diametric opposites, not including anything of the other. Our fear of the dark has been deeply ingrained. Dark — both literal and metaphorical — is bad, we are told. Stay away from it or suffer the consequences. Fight or reject every part of the darkness within you. Turn towards the light.

Despite the fact that science has shown that dark matter makes up most of the universe, our materialist culture has taught us to believe that darkness is the absence of everything. Where there is no light, there is nothing.

In the past century science has shown us that all particles come in pairs, positive and negative, and yet we humans have put a negative spin on the negative and tried to do away with its existence altogether. But energy naturally oscillates between these two poles, power moves in cycles, particles always have their twin.

Except in patriarchal culture. The man-made world is a strange, unnatural place where quasi-spiritual prejudice and ego-based fear trump reality it seems, in spite of the rhetorical claims of a love of rationality.

The light tends to be associated with *logos* — rationalism, logic, and order, and contrasted with the disorder and demonic qualities of the dark. The En-light-enment era (1620–1780) was a key development in Western civilisation as we know it today — a flowering of (white, masculine, Christian, Euro-centric) rationalist science, philosophy and politics. It was the blueprint for a masculine vision of the world, alongside a wholesale rejection of the Feminine and its associates: the irrational, the body, wild nature, the mad... All these were segregated as "Other". All needed to be controlled. The masculine approach to the dark, to anything that it perceives as threatening, has been to conquer and subjugate it, to force it into lightness, or lock it away. The end game of masculine power is the triumph of the ego over wildness, the chaos of the unconscious and shining the light of rational knowledge on all things. We see this in our ever-lit cities, in the domination of nature and darker skinned peoples by whites for hundreds of years. When darkness emerges through madness or rebellion, it has been brutally slain, medicated or confined.

For millennia this has been done in the name of the Father God of light. The Christian faith has instilled a spiritual fleeing from "the darkness" associated with the Devil and hell, to the dreamland of heaven, with Jesus, light of the world. But the Christians aren't alone in this. The Nazis, and more recently ISIS are playing out their own interpretations of masculine power and control.

Even the New Age movement has taken up this mission it seems — same message, different words. The new gurus have taught us to embrace our light bodies, shunning the darkness, and focusing purely on love and light, constant happiness and extreme optimism. But, as Karin L. Burke astutely points out: "In our efforts to feel better, many of us start shutting it off, in favor of pop psychology or easy spirituality. It's called spiritual bypass. It's an attempt to avoid painful feelings, unresolved issues, or developmental needs."

That is the basis of our culture as we know it — dismissing all that cannot be known with the rational mind. *Move towards the light, ignore the dark*, we are taught, again and again.

THE DARK ARTS OF THE PATRIARCHY

Despite claiming distaste and disbelief in witchcraft, our masculine culture has a powerful understanding of the dark arts. It's how they've kept their stranglehold on power for all this time. It is not that they are cleverer, stronger, divinely endowed or even in the majority, despite their claims to the contrary. It's that they use forms of mind and spiritual control, more subtle, but not that much less powerful, than the overt violence we stood witness to in the last section. The dark arts are psychological reminders of the real violence that can be played out without warning on our bodies and minds. But because they are invisible, and take place in the shadows, they are a more insidious form of control and when confronted can easily be denied, laughed off or turned back on the recipient as crazy imaginings.

Some of the most common of the dark arts of coercion that are commonly used in our culture include:

› Fear

› Shame, humiliation, embarrassment, discrediting difference as "madness"

› Controlling bodies—through strict dress codes, veiling, starvation. . .

› Banishment or threat of banishment

› Rewards. . . and threats

› Repression and dissociation

› Imposing hierarchy and clear authority

› Keeping people small, powerless, impoverished and infantilised

› Exhaustion and lack of adequate rest or recovery time

› Unattainable standards

› A focus on the external

› Closely policed spiritual and sexual experience

As a trained teacher, I recognise that we were taught many of these in our arsenal of control. As a parent I know that all mainstream parenting advice centres round them too. These are the tools of coercion, the rules of play in the patriarchy. Naturally they are the back bone of most patriarchal religions.

First they are used against us by authority figures when we are younger, when they are physically more powerful than us, and can enforce them. Then we learn to internalise them, creating a super-ego, or internal authority figure which continues the job on their behalf.

Each of these weapons in the arsenal of dark arts is a complex energy trap, taking our natural power and turning it against ourselves in a deadly game of self-policing in order to survive.

Whilst the dark arts remain nameless and invisible they keep control of us: sticking to us like spiders' webs in the dark, confining our movements, filling us with unconscious fears of what might happen next.

Each of these dark arts works to activate fear within us. The fear of being found out, the fear of being shamed, the fear of rejection, the fear of pain, the fear of loss of freedom or finances, the fear of abandonment and the ultimate fear — the fear of death.

FEAR

When I dare to be powerful—to use my strength in the service of my vision—then it becomes less and less important whether I am afraid.
Audre Lorde

Every so often, when you've come into fear, you've walked away. What if today you held that tremble, and stepped into the centre of it? What if today, you allow yourself more courage than you've ever felt? What if you did it anyway?
Sukhvinder Sircar

He's after me. I want to take my children to the top of the tall tower, but the old male guard at the bottom stands inscrutable and impotent in his uniform with his machine gun by his side. I run past him and up the stairs, it is the only way through to the other side, my daughters run behind me. But as I turn a corner of the spiral staircase a young man with dark curls, aims his gun and shoots, the bullet whistles past the side of my face, I can feel the cold air and hot metal, I run up the stairs in twos, he's after me, and then I'm trapped, at the top. I can see where I'm headed, the landscape opens up before me. But there is no way down from here.

He has me cornered, I cannot move, I try to scream but nothing comes out. My heart pounds, the air is being squeezed from my lungs, I have to get away. I scream again, he is getting closer. My eyes jam open as I feel a hand.

"It's OK, Lucy, you're safe," my husband murmurs, half awake, familiar with this routine when fear wakes me in the night, its dark tentacles winding round my neck, my belly, paralyzing me in my bed. The shadows in the room take on a life of their own and begin to move towards me like the dark pursuer from my dreams. I lie awake in the darkness trying to will myself to think of other things.

*

This is how women have lived for as long as they can remember. One eye always over our shoulders on the shadows in the dark — in our waking lives as well as our dreams. This is the ever-present shadow of fear.

We run and hide from the rapist, the murderer, the evil king, the robber, the terrorist, the sadist, the stalker, the vampire, the troll, he who wishes to do us harm, he who we fear. Again and again we run and hide from him, we are killed and raped, we are saved or sacrificed.

We may have met the dark man in real life — in the form of a rapist, abuser, cruel physician or burglar — he who intrudes, who penetrates without permission. He who deems us powerless, who abuses his greater physical strength and shames us into silence. Fear scrambles our signals — disconnecting us from ourselves, others and the life force, awakening trauma, shutting down our bodies, our feelings, or making us disregard our own safety, and open ourselves to anyone. Fear is the death force in energy form.

As Burning Women we learn again and again to face fear, and to see it for what it is. Not a shut cage door or a jail cell. . . but a portal of transformation. As Burning Women we learn again and again to stand in the face of fear, and feel it, rather than run or hide or capitulate. In feeling it fully we find our way through to the other side.

The dark arts work in the man-made world, simply because we believe their truth which we have been taught since birth: that the world is man-made and the power lies outside of us, in the grips of an omnipotent masculine force.

But it is not. It does not.

The way of Burning Woman is an unveiling of another truth, a deeper truth: our own truth. But to find it we have to have the courage to walk through the other side of fear.

In the psychic realm, the dark man represents our subconscious fears of masculine power that we have yet to make our peace with. Our dreams are often the first place we can practice witnessing and confronting our subconscious fears and transforming the power dynamic we have with the masculine. We can learn to develop healthy boundaries with him, learn to stand our ground, to roar in his face, to say *no*. We can also learn to partner him, play with him, take calculated risks, help him to transform. Our dreams are a physically safe training ground for the maturing Feminine psyche coming into her power.

In our dream life we can recognise that our attacker, our predator, is actually a part of ourselves, one that longs to share in our power, or express aspects of ourselves that we have cut off. However, as the immature masculine he does not know how to be in partnership, and so he grabs and threatens. Soon we learn that he is magnetised to us by our fear: the more we fear him, the bigger and stronger he grows. Whereas when we learn to stand our ground, rather than run in terror, to look him in the eye and to name him, then he loses his power over us.

We can then take this dream learning out into the waking world with us to confront our fears of stepping into our power. So that when as we do our work in the world, we have the tools to begin to disentangle fear's fingers from our guts. We know that fear is merely a shadow, that we, not it, hold the power.

But, as we get closer to our goals in the real world, we start to hear our fears in stereo: reading criticisms of our work, being attacked or threatened by rivals, facing rejection from those we love and respect. And we know that if we step back, if we walk away it will stop. But we will lose. And so we find ourselves, once again, caught between our inner burning and the outer burning.

To stand our ground in the face of such terror feels more than we can bear. I am there right now. If you read this book, it is because I have dared to walk through a fire so large I knew it would consume me.

This fear is strong. But so are we. And it knows something that we do not: when we dare to face it, we can free ourselves. But to do that we have to pass through the fire *whilst feeling fully*—we must consciously walk through the burning wall of oblivion, knowing that it may destroy everything we love.

Fire burns our worldly attachments, and shows us our most primal selves—our love and our fear—and asks us which we choose.

SHAME

No longer believe the shame, it is a lie you whisper to yourself to keep yourself small and you are so far from small, you are a magnificent human being. We may need to endure the terror of exposing our own magnificence. It is true that to begin with it might feel deeply uncomfortable to be seen, but it is time, tender one, hiding in the shadows, to offer love to your own un-livedness, to become the safe place to land your heart in the world, with its vast medicine bundle of beauty.

Lucy Pierce, *Belonging*

Shame corrodes the very part of us that believes we are capable of change.

Brené Brown,
I Thought It Was Just Me: Women Reclaiming Power and Courage in a Culture of Shame

Shame.

Slaps round the face.

Cuts like a knife.

Burns in your throat and makes your skin crawl.

Raw agony of flayed flesh

The braying mob look on and jeer.

And then silence so visceral you could bury yourself in it.

The patriarchal system is built on honour and reputation — saving face.

What is *face*? It is the persona or mask we have acquired as defence structure against a world we perceive — or have been told — is dangerous. It is how we cover our vulnerabilities.

When the patriarchal system refers to defending honour, it really means defending the persona—the projected, public self and reputation—without which we cannot function effectively within the System. Shame shatters the persona and destroys honour, it does this by homing in on a fundamental truth of ours, which we perceive as dangerous and unacceptable to others, and yet is fundamental to our existence. It reveals that which we have purposely tried to conceal: shame is the slipping of the mask to reveal a vulnerable, fallible human underneath. Shame makes us bad and wrong for who we are and what we love.

Shame is a pilot light that warns us when we are approaching the boundary for acceptability: it is a cultural tracking device to keep us within the fold. Which is good, if the community supports our health and growth. But if that culture is stunting us, or wishing us harm, then shame is a faulty warning light, trying to make us conform to values we no longer hold, and an authority we no longer respect.

Shame is the key tool in the arsenal of the repression of Feminine power. It is the enemy of pleasure. The drier up of juices—creative and sexual. The putter-on of clothes. Shame says: *Who do you think you are? What will people think? You dirty little whore, you untalented piece of shit, you pretentious arse, you stupid woman.* Shame says: *Sit still, shut up and do not embarrass yourself. You are bad, and you will be exposed. Shame on you, shame on you, shame on you.*

It is a spell of disempowerment and disconnection that is cast upon us early—magic words which make us believe: if I am not perfect, if I am vulnerable, if I am complex, then I am wrong and deserve to be alone, to die. I am not acceptable. I am different. I do not belong. I have no rights. No authority.

As women we have internalised its messages, which we have received so many times, in so many ways. *We are inherently not okay.* Shame confirms this loud and clear.

I understand the power of shame. I have believed these voices so many times. I have seen others be pulled into their web in a thousand different vicious ways. Over the past couple of years, I have begun to see more clearly every time that shame engages me: shame about what my body looks like; what others think of my work; asking for what I want sexually; shame for not being a good enough mother; shame about not having enough money, about having too much; shame for being sick all the time; for having a dirty house and for having a cleaner; for painting unacceptable art; for not being patient enough; for being a bad daughter... the list is endless. And it is truly disabling.

Burning Woman learns to overcome the crippling effects of shame and fear by realizing that they are universal patriarchal control patterns: **they are not personal**, even though they are always couched in personal terms. They say everything about the one who speaks them, not the one being shamed. When she learns this, she cracks the code and breaks the spell of the patriarchal power matrix. She learns to release herself from the shadow power of the father's stories, and reconnect directly with the full power of the Feminine source energy.

If the empowered Feminine could be described in one word it would be: shameless. The Feminine is she whose ways cannot be proscribed or controlled, she who follows her own flow, she who knows that her vulnerability is the birthplace of real power.

As good quasi-men of the patriarchy, we have been told that vulnerability is weakness. Vulnerability allows soft spots for others to exploit and attack. Vulnerability=death. But in the Feminine model of power, vulnerability is a key strength. It allows meaningful connection, empathy and authentic expression—which all human beings naturally seek.

Vulnerability is the birthplace of love, belonging, joy, courage, empathy, and creativity. It is the source of hope, empathy, accountability, and authenticity. If we want greater clarity in our purpose or deeper and more meaningful spiritual lives, vulnerability is the path.
Brené Brown, *Daring Greatly*

The deeper in shame we are the more we are disconnected from ourselves, our community and the world beyond us. Shame occurs in and cultivates isolation and disconnection. So to be defused, it needs to be shared. We need to be witnessed in our naked truth to expose our shame.

So here is the magic: if you do not define yourself by the System's rules, if you surround yourself with others who do not buy into their values, then you are free. Completely. To be yourself. Your full self, not just the self that you feel safe projecting into the world, but your shadow side too, the parts of you that you have always had to hide in order to be honourable.

The first, most important step into power is through the portal of fear and shame: uncasting their spells and having the courage to stand face to face with your own power. When you do this, you step from pouring all your energy into appeasing a monolithic structure that will never accept you, however hard you try, one that will always change the boundaries and demand more, to one which sees and loves you as you are.

You have reached the threshold of the portal of Feminine power.

Dare you cross over?

4

THE THRESHOLD

A woman's initiation includes many moments of crossing a threshold. This threshold is the bridge to our feminine soul, and crossing over is the beginning of becoming.

Sue Monk Kidd

Where do we go, when we don't know where to go?

How do we get to where we do not know?

Welcome. I see you there, standing on the threshold. Step further into the darkness, into your own darkness. Follow the sound of my voice. You cannot see me. You have no need for your outer eyes and ears here.

Here you are. Alone. But not alone.

I am here for you, holding space, waiting with you.

This is the space between dreaming and becoming. The liminal space. The held breath.

For perhaps the first time in your life you are standing in a space which is not defined in any way by the masculine. This is No Man's Land. The threshold where time and space coalesce in a different way and we re-emerge in a new identity. Here we come to reclaim our words, our images, our spirits, our souls. Here is where we meet our Feminine power.

Rest here. Allow the shadow space to embrace you in your wholeness. Here you lie in the womb of infinite possibilities. Here you can let go of your projections, your personas, your stories. Lay them down and allow yourself to rest. Know yourself without limits. Get intimate with your essence.

This is the place of creativity. The passing place of life and death. Where existence flits in and out between pure consciousness and the material realm.

Settle in, make yourself at home.

Time does not apply here. Only truth. You cannot hurry this place. It is the resting space of eternity. This is the space you must inhabit to hear the call, the whisper of your soul, the shouts of She. This is the space which always holds the sacred invitation to healing, becoming. This is where your invitation to dance in the flames can always be found.

This is the place you will return to time and again.

Are you willing to wait in the space between stories? To sink into the warm depths of yourself and listen without agenda?

Behind the fear, the planning, the cleverness and noise. Behind it all. The invitation is waiting for you; the call is sounding.

Can you hear it? Are you listening?

Can you feel it? Are you here?

5

THE FEMININE DARK

We need to dream the dark as process, and dream the dark as change, to create the dark in a new image. Because the dark creates us.

Lauren, in Starhawk's *Dreaming the Dark*

There is an underlying longing for darkness. It's as important as sleep. It feels natural for us, as humans born from wombs, to search for a home or understanding that is based on feeling and connection rather than sight.

Eila Kundrie Carrico, *The Other Side of the River*

Darkness is the ancient womb. Night-time is womb-time. Our souls come out to play. The darkness absolves everything; the struggle for identity and impression falls away.

John O'Donohue, *Anam Cara*

Soft and warm,
A mother's nest, feathered with softest down,
A dark cocoon in the palm of the goddess,
I am held, so gently,
My skin is night, and the stars my necklace.
I am safe, I am home, I am loved, I can rest.

Can you try to picture a softer dark than the masculine dark you have been brought up with? A darkness which is benevolent and mysterious? Feel yourself cradled in it. Fully held. Can you imagine that rather than a void of nothingness, darkness holds complete intelligence and possibility—waiting to take form.

I invite you to step into that darkness with me, and adjust your gaze, heightening your vision, learning to see through sound, hear through feeling. In the dark you need all your senses. As you wait in the dark, your inner eyes and inner ears are heightened and aware, your instincts are strong. Your ears are primed, the hairs on your skin stand up. You are fully alive. Fully alert. In the darkness you are here.

This is not the darkness of fear, but of love. Deep, complete, unconditional acceptance. The loving darkness of our mother's womb. Soft and dark and round and safe, the darkness that held us as we grew. Our earthly bodies did not come from a masculine God but a real human female's belly. For the first part of our life, we were at home within her. We belonged, intimately, within the Feminine. And part of us longs to return to that safety, ease and feeling of deep belonging.

But for many women even their womb time was not a time of safety. For those of us with mother wound issues, attachment issues, who have been adopted, have lost, or never had the experience of a deep, safe, loving connection to the Feminine during their lifetime, the Feminine dark presents deeper challenges. Estranged from the flesh and blood mother, systemically disconnected from the patriarchal system, having stepped away from the Father God we can find ourselves adrift and alone. We become all the more aware of the strict prohibitions on the divine feminine, our lack of connection to real flesh and blood women, and find we have nowhere safe to belong. Nowhere to rest and be held.

We have died to our old selves, but do not know who we will be. How can we find ourselves at home in the Feminine when we have felt homeless, rootless, disintegrated all our lives? How can we know Her when we do not know Her?

Start by having the courage to simply be here in the dark, without filling it with stories. Learn to know it intimately, personally.

Allow yourself to be held within the matrix, the womb space of the divine.

> *The Creation Mother is always the Death Mother and vice versa. Because of this dual nature, or double-tasking, the great work before us is to learn to understand what around and about us and what within us must live, and what must die. Our work is to apprehend the timing of both; to allow what must die to die, and what must live to live.*
>
> **Clarissa Pinkola Estés, Women Who Run With the Wolves**

Within the course of our lives we pass through a thousand deaths, losses big and small — of identities and loved ones, places and people. Our death and rebirth to the Feminine is one of the biggest.

Through this experience we learn the truth that death never is The End, but always leads to rebirth, and new existence in a different form. We discover that what we had feared as final annihilation is actually an integral part of the creative process. This helps us to release our fear and resistance, and begin to lean into the divine paradox, embracing the reality that in death lies life, in creativity lies destruction.

When we do, what emerges is the freedom to fully and creatively engage with the miracle that is life, bringing the full power which lies within us into the world, during our brief journey from the womb of our mother to the womb of the Earth.

To come into our wisdom, we have to step into the Feminine dark once more. To face the shadows we have run from and integrate them. We need the balance of the dark —

the unknown, the mystery, the veiled, the uncontrolled and unnameable, madness and chaos, stillness and silence, winter and night. This place of renewal, death, and birth is our soul's home.

Any time we recapture this primal womb darkness, we get to experience ourselves as safe, precious, held and cared for, free from striving or asserting ourselves. We simply get to be. We rest in our essence, connected to ourselves and everything beyond us. We experience firsthand the pulsing of life within us: our raw Feminine power.

And the longer we dare to spend in the dark, we begin to see that it is never truly dark — there are stars, and there is the moon. We learn to be guided by these subtler lights. As well as our own inner senses. We learn to trust the wisdom of other ways of knowing when the light is dim.

The dark is the crucible of transformation. It is a vital part of us, and we of it. When we wake up to the dark and face what frightens us then we can begin to make magic.

INITIATIONS INTO DARKNESS

Initiation into the mysteries of life entails walking the great labyrinth. The first part of the journey is finding your way in, past the meanders and distractions that could lead you astray, until you find the centre, the heart, where lie all the answers about yourself. But that is only the beginning. Once you have absorbed the sacred knowledge, then starts the second leg of the journey, which is finding your way back out, carrying the insights that you gained as you were staring into the intense light of your soul.
Nicole Schwab, *The Heart of the Labyrinth*

The darkness is

An invitation to intimacy

With that we have never seen or heard,

But which we know as truth.

An invitation beyond the doors of perception

To the deepest layers of our soul

Unsullied by the dust of the world.

In many traditions a key part of a woman's initiation is to be left alone in nature, often immersed in total darkness — whether sleeping out by herself under the stars, finding her way through a wood or descending into the depths of a cave. This gives her a lived experience of confronting of her learned and instinctive fears, teaching her how to dig deep into her own resources and discover both her vulnerability and deep strength. In the darkness we can confront our own shadows and the fears that we project, and learn to listen to the instincts that protect us from real dangers.

Our early experiences of the dark can deeply influence our sense of safety, or lack of safety, throughout our adult lives. In the dark our senses are wide open, we are more vulnerable, hyper-aroused, and so whatever happens to us there will stay with us. Initiations in the dark are initiations of the soul.

Growing up in a culture without such rites of passage, my initiations to the dark have been unguided. Some beautiful, some terrifying, all totally unexpected. I hold them dear as some of the most profound and powerfully memorable experiences of my life.

When I was five years old I had two very different initiations into the darkness. One of love, and one of fear. The first, I was taken by my mother to a Midsummer ceremony on a village green. The event has taken on a magical place in my memory:

shadowy figures and flickering flaming torches reflected in the mirror-still lake. Which was real and which merely a reflection? I could hardly tell. It seemed as though two worlds had, for a moment in time, found their way back to each other. Under cover of darkness the veil had lifted. The darkness was bigger and wider and richer than all the people and the music that adorned it. It was alive. Fully alive. It was in me and I was in it, and it was so beautiful.

The initiation of fear happened that same year. It was the most turbulent part of my childhood, filled with trauma and deep instability. An ex-boyfriend of my mother's broke into our house one night and hid in the cupboard in the hallway. I remember her coming into my room, waking me up and pulling me downstairs, down through the internal staircase, through the front door of the house below and up the street, barefoot in the dark until we found sanctuary in a neighbour's house. It was as scary as it sounds. And burned vividly into my memory.

These were my early initiations into the two possibilities of darkness, the masculine and the Feminine. The dark in which I as a girl was prey and the one in which magic could happen. For years the fear won, but the seed of the beautiful dark had been planted.

Soft velvet black
You cradle me
Until I am dissolved into a billion
Pin points of light.

On the eve of my thirty-fifth birthday, Midsummer's Eve, I was on my way back from our women's book club. Though it was well after eleven, there was still a streak of sunset on the horizon. The evening was balmy, so unusual for the south coast of Ireland, and so I went to lie on the grass and watch the last vestiges of light recede and wait for the darkness. At first there were just two stars visible, plus the bright orbs of Venus and Jupiter, but slowly, slowly, as darkness spread, the full display of stars emerged. Three-dimensional pinpoints of light, millions of years old, beaming in from across the galaxy. The silence was as deep as the darkness, I grabbed a blanket, wrapped myself in it, cocooned like a caterpillar, and watched the stars till I fell asleep.

Never in my thirty-five years had I slept alone on the grass under the stars. I had been too busy, too scared, too worried about cold or discomfort. But in writing this book I realised I needed to readjust my relationship with the dark. It was thrilling, for the first couple of hours, to sleep in the open air. But then I woke with a jolt. A crack of twigs. Something moving close by. My heart pounded and my mind envisaged rapists and murderers. I froze and tried to wait out my terror, but eventually headed inside. The masculine dark had won once more. But the magic of the dark, the need to heal the trauma of my past became more insistent than ever.

And so began my more frequent freely chosen visits with the dark, my self-initiations — walking home in the dark, moonlit walks on the beach and dark bedroom retreats.

As Burning Women, I realised, we need to find regular ways of both accessing, and moving through, dark liminal spaces, to experience them not as places of powerlessness, but instead of infinite potential, as training grounds for the soul. Looking back, I realised I had been subconsciously seeking out the dark Feminine for most of my adult life.

My first memory of this was in Japan in my early twenties when I was living and working there with my fiancé. Kyoto is a veritable tourist mecca and not the sort of place you would expect to have an intimate initiation into the dark. But the dark has funny ways of surprising us.

The nation's capital for over a thousand years, Kyoto is a

vibrant modern city built on ancient foundations, a metropolis of twenty-four-hour karaoke bars and pinball parlours, with their dazzling flashing lights and hypnotic noise, dense traffic and towering neon signs. But it is also a city of thousand-year-old temples, palaces and gardens of simple zen beauty. Kiyomizu is perhaps the best known of all the Kyoto temples, a three-storey pagoda overlooking a mountainside of cherry blossom. But there, before you go in to the main attraction, is a smaller shrine, where the Japanese clap their hands to ward off evil spirits in front of an altar overhung with strings of prayers. There, if you know where to look, is a small doorway into an ancient practice.

A monk in robes greets you with a deep bow. You press your coins into his hand, and follow the passage which takes you down a gentle slope, your hand on a rope, the simple stone walls gradually receding as the path spirals ever-deeper below the temple, into what feels like the womb of the Earth. Enveloped in darkness, the only sensory orientation you have is the muffled sound of slow shuffling steps of the visitors ahead and behind. And the pounding of your own heart. And the rope in your hand. And nothingness. Thick, dark, black, nothingness.

Though it only lasts less than a minute before you touch the centre stone and spiral back out, time seems to have no place in the darkness. It is eternal and all-consuming. It is thrilling, terrifying and deeply soothing all at once. You experience the ecstasy of the dark: stepping beyond your worldly limitations, and into a fuller sense of self.

Emerging blinking into the light I longed to hand over more coins and re-enter the darkness. To step in each time more consciously and courageously, to face my fear time and again until I knew it intimately.

Another more recent encounter with the darkness was in the south of France, on holiday with my family, soul sister and her boy. We stayed in the foothills of the Pyrénées where Neolithic people had painted cave walls tens of thousands of years before. Our first stop on our impromptu pilgrimage into the Earth was a long cave, the Mas D'Azil, where a river —and now the road — disappear abruptly into the side of the hill, and suddenly, there you are, a tiny human cell in the great womb of Gaia, the rushing waters filling your ears, like embryonic fluid: so deeply soothing and comforting.

Onwards we travelled to more caves, this time a complex network over a hundred metres under the ground, with a dark river running through the subterranean chasm. I remember my legs shaking as we were led down the steep, slippery steps carved into the cave wall, clinging on for dear life to the rickety iron handrail. *If I slip here I could die,* my mind played on loop. Death walked just one step ahead of me. I tried to keep my eyes on the steps, and from the vertiginous bone-shattering drop below. We arrived at the bottom and embarked on the wobbly boats. Our guide began to pull us along, warning us when to duck down, as we levelled ourselves with the sides of the boat to get through the tightest gaps.

Stalactites and stalagmites were artfully picked out with coloured lights. . . until we reached a section that was unlit, and we glided in silence in the darkness, through the narrow stone chasm, the birth canal of the Goddess. Once again that feeling emerged, which you can only know in complete darkness: the thrill, the terror, the absolute peace. The total absence of being which is eternity.

JOURNEYS TO THE UNDERWORLD

The demons who attempt to block the gateways to the deep spaces
of the [inner] realm often take ghostly/ghastly forms, comparable
to noxious gases not noticeable by ordinary sense perception. Each
time we move into deeper space, these numbing ghostly gases work
to paralyze us, to trap us so that we will be unable to move further.
Each time we succeed in overcoming their numbing effect, more
dormant senses come alive.
Mary Daly, *Gyn/Ecology*

Two days later I had another sort of initiation to darkness when
the dark mind unleashed. It was as though a pin had burst my
bubble. Everything was darkness and despair. I felt detached,
alone, despised. Everyone hated me. I hated me even more.
Dark thoughts ran unceasingly through my head. I looked out
the window at the breath-taking mountain view, snow-capped
in the dazzling July sunshine. At the faces of my children
laughing in the sun. Nothing. I felt nothing. It was as though
a gauze curtain had been drawn between me and the world. Its
beauty could not touch me. It was just me and the darkness in
my head. Nothing else could find its way in. I slapped myself
around the face to try and shake myself out of it, then collapsed
in a puddle of tears on the bathroom floor longing for death.

*

Initiations to the darkness can be exhilarating, or terrifying,
depending on when and how they happen, how prepared we
are and how supported we are during the process. Often the
initiations do not happen in a tourist cave or festival, but in
the recesses of our own minds, with terrors and chasms of
emptiness far more real than anything we have seen on Earth.
They remind us that transformation can be dangerous and
requires enormous courage.

When we don't consciously initiate the body and mind into

the dark, it can force itself on us chaotically and destructively instead. We can see this in our culture as a prevalence of mental illness and dissociative disorders.

Our bodies can initiate us into the darkness when we lose control for a moment through illness, stress or exhaustion, and become unable to function in the masculine sphere. But rather than follow this path into the darkness we put our focus on trying to do 'normal', patching up the cracks, medicating ourselves, rather than by supporting the break-through process which is occurring. And so the process becomes more severe, and we are taken kicking and screaming down into the underworld which can be terrifying... and deadly. In the underworld we come face to face with the flip side of our creative power: the death urge, and the shadow side of our vision: our fear.

We fear the descent of madness or depression, because in the masculine view of the dark, they lead us away from the light, through complete disintegration (lack of control) and towards the ultimate darkness: death and hell. Whereas the dark mind when seen through the lens of Feminine darkness offers a different perspective: the underworld as a place between the worlds, where healing and transformation can happen. Disintegration is a necessary step to greater integration.

Often we long for "spiritual" experiences to "raise our consciousness" or "empower" us, but when they come they are very different to what we expect. We have been led to expect that spiritual experiences are when we are touched by the light and transformed. When actually far more spiritual experience takes place in the dark. A cursory flick through the stories of spiritual transformation in any of the major sacred texts will quickly show you that the road to spiritual power is littered with trials, exile, infertility, loss, disability, wrestling angels and wandering in the desert.

Each breaking open, each initiation into the underworld through grief, illness, depression, anxiety or loss—is a potential initiation, a portal of possibility where we get the chance to see and feel the very root of our own fire in the deepest dark. In this place we get to see our inner spark more clearly, as we are detached from our daily busyness and sense of belonging. We get to move further inwards, to let go of the shells of ourselves, and break open our self-concept to include our fuller selves.

But most of us see the darkness approach and freeze, we feel true terror in the face of what feels like the dead zone, and we do everything we can to resist it, to run the other way, to medicate it, numb ourselves, distract ourselves... Walking into inner space requires an ability to be with the darkness, to discern, to listen deeply and to move beyond our fear, into a trust of the process of disintegration, into a deep surrender to it. Learning to be in the dark requires that we learn to hold space for ourselves. And find others who can hold space for us as we journey.

In the dark we are not defined by our exterior —we are not defined by our beauty or bodily appearance, our money or worldly power which our culture tells us are important. We become formless and fluid as our masks fall to the floor.

Entering the dark, we peel away the layers of false selves and identities so that our authentic, inner Feminine power can shine.

GOING DARK

You, darkness, that I come from
I love you more than all the fires
that fence in the world,
for the fire makes a circle of light for everyone
and then no one outside learns of you.

But the darkness pulls in everything —
shapes and fires, animals and myself,
how easily it gathers them! —
powers and people —

and it is possible a great presence is moving near me.

I have faith in nights.

Rainer Maria Rilke

I invite you to step with trust and courage into the Feminine darkness. Let go of your persona, your worldly identities, and experience yourself intimately as an integral part of the endless darkness, the sea of infinite creative potential. The more you know yourself in this way, the more rooted in your source power you will be. And the less power the world — its threats, judgements and controls — will exert on you.

Total darkness is rare in this era of electric lighting inside and out, car headlights, glowing smart phones and computer screens constantly vying for our attention. Bright light activates the neo-cortex (the newest part of the brain, responsible for complex thought, the home of *logos*), it also stimulates adrenalin production. Whereas in safe, dark places the body produces oxytocin, melatonin and other hormones which allow us access to the more primal parts of the brain, and promote feelings of deep relaxation and ease.

Going dark is an important regular practice for Burning Women. It serves to disconnect us from the outer world, from the racing, chattering mind and incessant doing, and reconnect with self/Source. We fully recharge and revitalise when we allow ourselves to go dark. We allow space for our embers to glow more brightly, so that we can truly sense what we burn for and focus on how we can become further inflamed with it. In the dark we come out of our comfort zones, out of our minds and into our primal bodies — sounds, thoughts, feelings take on different dimensions. As creatives our job is to uncover what lies in the shadows, and give it new identity, new life. As healers our job is to identify what lurks in the shadows and heal or integrate it.

A number of Burning Women I know choose to 'go dark' regularly. Stepping away from technology and distractions, they immerse themselves in nature and their own creative impulses undistracted. Be it by living off-grid for a day each week, or even months or years. By returning to writing by hand, and living by firelight and candlelight for the winter season or just winter solstice. By retreating every time their menstrual blood emerges, or on their personal Sabbath, or simply when they choose to create.

But be warned, sister: in the dark the mind usually goes through its bag of tricks. In the darkness the mind is not our friend. The power that it believes it has in the man-made world of *logos* does not work — and once it sees that, it can freak out, trying to order and control. And when it can't, it panics. It projects its own shadows, terrors and imaginings. It churns around chattering on and making you believe its stories.

The first way to find ease in the dark is to quiet the mind, perhaps through breathing techniques or mindfulness practice. In the daylight we believe we are our thoughts and that they are reality. In the dark we learn that we have the choice to listen to and believe our thoughts. We learn that they are a river running over the top of a deep dark chasm of being. We are not the river. We do not control the river. It takes consistent practice and unlearning.

We are not taught how to deal with the process of inner transformation, or recognise what is happening in the dark. But our souls are pushing us to go dark. . . so that they can emerge more fully.

Transformation cannot and will not ever happen by mental force or in the realm of the mind. But this is our comfort zone, and so this is where we try to, believe we can, make it happen. Transformation happens in the dark zone. It requires that we walk into the dark, away from everything that makes us feel safe and defines us.

Entering the darkness requires that we acknowledge that we are not just our minds, nor can our minds help us. We need to learn to walk without the light of the mind, to stay calm without word knowledge. In the darkness we learn that surrender is our ally, feeling our guide and resistance our biggest enemy. We have to learn to trust another power — something deeper and more primal.

The dark speaks in a Feminine voice. And She calls us to listen.

WOMB SPACE — FEMININE HEART OF DARKNESS

We bleed. We burn. We are powerful.
Jackie Stewart

Ovarian energy is a woman's creative fire energy. It is the energetic source of life force energy utilised in making children, as well as making any creation a woman brings into the world.
Tami Lynn Kent, *Wild Feminine*

The voice of the dark, the voice of the womb, is a voice long forgotten, but once contacted it becomes a staunch ally and your inner guide. This is more than the voice of your intuition; this is the voice of your Feminine essence, where you birth and create from, where you learn again and again to surrender. It is the centre of your unique power as a woman.

The womb is the Feminine heart of darkness. A dark space of seemingly infinite creativity. It lies at the very core of our physical being and yet most of us will never see it. It is a place we can only penetrate through feeling and intuition, with our inner eyes.

The womb is considered by many healing systems to be the central node of the female energy system. In yogic traditions, it lies at the heart of the second chakra. It is often referred to as a woman's second heart. Many believe it to be central to all her creative functions—not just her fertility, but also her visioning and artistic abilities. It is said to be a crucible for her powers, and where a woman's sexual energy is coiled.

However, in Western medicine this uniquely female organ has traditionally been perceived as capricious and far more trouble than it's worth. The cause of "women's problems", Western science and medicine have never really felt at ease with the womb throughout their history, and their focus has only been on its reproductive functions. Or rather dysfunctions.

In the past it was considered to wander aimlessly around the female body, causing symptoms of hysteria, a solely female complaint, diagnosed by male doctors, which affected vast swathes of the female population. In the US today the two most common surgeries are both female only, and on the womb: C-sections and hysterectomies. [xxxiii]

In the Western world pre-menstrual syndrome, the most common of women's womb sufferings, has reached epidemic proportions. According to the US Government's National Women's Health Information Center, three out of every four adult women experience symptoms during their childbearing years, with 30-40% suffering impairment of daily activity and 3-7% experiencing severe, disabling symptoms.

Our wombs have been screaming in their own language of pain and dis-ease that patriarchal culture is strangling them. They are suffering. We are suffering. This culture is not healthy for us or our bodies. Our immense Feminine power is being stifled into cysts and tumours and cramps. It is trapped. Life is not flowing as it should. Our wombs are telling us of the abuse, if we would only listen. Our wombs are trying to bring our attention to our Feminine place of power.

> *At her first bleeding a woman meets her power.*
> *During her bleeding years she practices it.*
> *At menopause she becomes it.*
> **Traditional Native American saying**

Every month between our early teens and early fifties, we receive a powerful monthly womb initiation into the different faces of the Feminine: our creative and destructive powers. It is a gift that we are not taught to treasure in our culture, instead we tend to ignore, resent and resist it. We are taught to hide it away: *don't talk about it, don't let it show.* Our bleeding is seen not as our power, but as shameful weakness.

As Burning Women, our menstrual cycle is one of our key navigation tools and sources of power and health. It helps us to find and live within the regular rhythm which is seen throughout nature — that of moving endlessly between darkness and light, birth and death. Our bleeding is intimately connected to our burning.

During ovulation it is our energetic powerhouse and where the Masculine and Feminine merge together to form new life. Pre-menstrually we tap into our firepower—our ability to rage and destroy. At menstruation and gestation, the womb is where we learn to rest in the Feminine dark within ourselves and embody our understanding of holding space.

Our menstrual period naturally brings us to this place. A place that we are often scared to go. A place we cannot enter with our minds, but only through our bodies. The greatest gift of our moon time is in learning to clear space and enter the darkness, in order to be reborn as fertile, creative beings once more. We learn that this letting go, this cocooning in the darkness, is integral to our health. Again and again we must learn to be comfortable in the formlessness of transformation, and rest in the mystery.

Month by month we are taught that our power is not based on possessions or external prestige, but something far deeper and stronger: our power is a natural force, intimately connected to the force of nature, and rooted in our bodies.

Our power is the power of life itself.

And it is innate to us.

THE UNCONSCIOUS

Becoming our fullest selves is a journey of the soul: mythical, magical, transformative. It requires of us to surface from the depths of our psyches what we may not want to see, know or feel, what we may want to reject. It is precisely our hidden grief, unspoken rage, fear, longing and unknown joy that wants to know of us our courage. Are we brave enough to own its existence within us and not exile it to places we refuse to go? You say that you want to be whole and free? First then, descend. Find the gold hidden in the dark caves of your heart and belly. This is your rite of passage home. When you truly know all of who you are, you will no longer live in avoidance and fear of your vast human nature.
ALisa Starkweather

In we go, deeper and deeper. Through the body and into consciousness itself.

The dark is a place of few words and many images. Where our worst fears and brightest dreams lie hidden, formless and nameless, waiting to be discovered. This is a realm we have been warned of in stories—the underworld, the dark wood, the black night, the stormy ocean, the underground river, the locked box —the place of demons and witches. This is No Man's Land, the place our culture has taught us to fear and turn from. This is the realm of the unconscious where *logos* is not king. This is the domain of the Queen of Darkness, the Goddess.

The unconscious is a repository of immense wealth — of all the other possibilities of existence which are currently not part of our conscious functioning in the world. It is here, the personal and collective unconscious, that we descend to in our journeys in the dark.

We may access it intentionally through dreams, trance work, body work, poetry or painting. We may get here unwillingly through grief or depression. Through these portals to the underworld, strange visions beckon, images haunt us, whispers of words catch on the inner breeze, shadows of creatures we do not recognise. As things get stranger, we know we are getting closer to Source.

Often we have a tendency to skirt around the edges of these processes, to stay in safe, familiar territory, revisiting old ground, too scared of the consequences or what we might find if we go deeper and darker. We often try to make the images and ideas we find here acceptable, censoring or only partially expressing that which we have discovered, in order to make them identifiable with the persona we have dedicated ourselves to cultivating. On one level, this is wise — the unconscious contains many things that we fear hugely, that we have purposely repressed. It has the potential to awaken physical and emotional trauma, and to threaten our mental health and stability. Our discoveries have the capacity to destroy the control that we enjoy, and the calm, ordered world that we have created. If we are looking to sustain the status quo we need to keep the hell out of the unconscious.

However, playing safe and transformation do not work hand in hand. Transformation cannot be micromanaged. When we surrender to it, the rules of the ordinary world do not apply.

The experience can be guided, but never controlled. The whole point of exploring the unconscious, is that we do not know what we will find. This requires great courage.

It requires a leaving of the conscious mind: the home of the patriarchal system. It necessitates throwing down the rule book and entering with curiosity and daring. Each time we delve into our unconscious, each time we tap into sacred power, each time we move into our bodies, we are part of the revolution, we are locating new sources of power, identity, existence, passion, joy and possibility outside of the mind system. We are freeing ourselves from fear and shame and clothing ourselves in the flames of our own unique beings.

DREAMS AND VISIONS

If all the women of the world
recorded their dreams for a single week
and laid them all end to end,
we would recover
the last million years
of women's hymns and chants
and dances,
all of women's art and stories,
and medicines,
all of women's lost histories.
Clarissa Pinkola Estés

Dreams are a direct gateway to the unconscious, and one which we potentially have access to in the darkness of every night. If we choose to pay attention and commit to learning their language, they offer us great riches.

Whilst many of our dreams are simply a way for our brains to process the thoughts, events, people and places of the day, they can also carry direct communications from the divine, our primal instinctive selves and the personal and collective unconscious.

We all know the deeper sort of dreams that stay with us. Not just into the milky first light of morning, but with a technicolor vividness throughout our days and even our entire lives. These are the dreams I am talking about here. The dreams that make you call your mother to check she is okay. The dream in which you meet your unborn child. The dream that introduces you to your spirit animal. The dream that both my grandparents had on the same night, which led my grandfather to a bar in the local town, to meet the man who was to teach him about pottery, which has become a three-generation business. The dreams that share the whisperings of your soul and have the power to shape your life.

The night after I finished the first draft of this book, I had such a dream.

I leave my husband in his place of work, and walk past my son on my way home to my daughters, on the other side of the city. I am passed by flank after flank of blue dressed police, more police than I ever knew existed. "What's happening?" I ask.

"The Chinese have set an ultimatum, if we support the attacks on ISIS they will attack Wednesday morning," they tell me.

That is this morning. I look out to the bay and it is filled with warships of every size — from small dinghies to massive aircraft carriers with battered planes on the deck.

I enter a block of flats on my way, stopping in to visit an old wise man, much loved, but now impotently sat in his easy chair. I leave him, somewhat comforted, and join many others, out on the balcony: at least I will not be alone when death comes. We watch as our police shoot out into the hazy blue, and then in answer, an atomic explosion, ripping the clouds and seas, barrelling towards us. We fall to our knees, looking to see how safe the structure is above us, knowing we are dead any way. I feel absolute desolation at being apart from my family, at the loss of my family, of all these people with me, of the beautiful Earth and the places we have built. Absolute desolation that it has come to this. What a waste, what a tragedy.

At first I thought the dream was simply about the escalating war between Western governments and Islamic State, a reflection of the terror in the air after the terrorist attacks in Paris. Discussions of reprisals had filled the nightly news and the French had declared the attacks an act of war.

This is one of my greatest fears, as a child who grew up in the shadow of the nuclear age, at the end of the Cold War. A child of peace-loving parents who were engaged in their own personal nuclear holocaust. I have grown up terrified of conflict, of the possibility of the ordinary skies being filled, without warning, with the drone of war planes. I recognise that this is both a literal and metaphorical fear, the terror of the little Good Girl who makes a pact that if she is good, please God let there not be war today.

But then further interpretations came to me as I reflected more.

Interestingly in the dream I was just going home to see my daughters, my husband and son were the other side of the city, I was aware of this sense of leaving behind the masculine and moving into the Feminine. In the dream, this was represented spatially by a movement from the right hand side to the left (traditionally right-handedness is the correct, masculine way of imposing oneself on the world. I am, of course, a left-hander!)

On the way home I popped in to visit the Father God of my childhood, he was still there, but benign, no longer all-powerful.

And then there was the explosion. I realised that for me it correlated with the power of the Feminine — both my fear of my mother exploding in fury if I confronted her about our relationship dynamics, but also the immense wild, natural power of the divine Feminine. The ocean is a common symbol of the Feminine in dreamers' psyches, whereas architecture, especially tower blocks like the one I was in represent the phallus, or masculine—order and structure.

Despite my fear, the explosion was deeply beautiful. It came in response to the pathetic ejaculations of all the guards of the patriarchy firing in unison into the blue, like a shoal of fiery sperm. The response was silent but awesome: a bubble of pure power and energy coming straight towards me.

But whilst the architecture around me started to fall, I didn't die. The ending was left open. I just felt a wave of deep, deep grief for what had been lost. And a sense of having been somehow initiated further into the wild, uncontrollable power of the Feminine, which had blasted away the previous man-made structures of control.

I interpreted this dream as my psyche's way of communicating to me that vast blockages to the Feminine power—personal and collective—were in the process of being destroyed. It reflected exactly where I was in my life. I had struggled deeply with the first draft of this book, knowing that it was caught behind energetic blocks. Fears of speaking openly about the divine Feminine. Fears of speaking openly about the erotic. Fears of attack and reprisal for so blatantly critiquing the patriarchy. I was living what I was being asked to learn in deeper and deeper ways, but still it was not deep enough. Until I could clear these old blockages, the book could not flow. I needed to let the old structures crumble down, but I was not in it alone. The Feminine power coming through would help the process of clearing space. It was time to let go. It was time to surrender. I woke in terror for what had happened, in grief for what I had lost. . . and in awe-inspired beauty of the power of the Feminine erupting and the fact that I was here at this momentous time, to bear witness as it emerged into the world.

BURNING QUESTIONS & FIRESTARTERS

MASCULINE DARKNESS

What is your relationship to the darkness — now, as a younger woman, and as a child?

Do you believe you are alone in the dark? In danger? What are you afraid of? Can you allow yourself to picture it? Why does it threaten you so?

FEARS

Firestarter

Make a list of your fears.

Next to each note down what it is that created this fear in you, and when you learned it.

Can you go back in time and enter into dialogue with each of these fears, and reclaim your power from them?

SHAME

Firestarter

Make a list of your shames.

Next to each note down who it was that created this shame in you, when you learned it. Can you go back in time and enter into dialogue with each of these shames, and reclaim your power from them? Try to see them in their own shame and smallness and allow compassion for them to emerge.

Firestarter

Dress yourself in many, many layers of clothing, each representative of a key shame. Look at yourself in a full length mirror, how do you look? Reflect on how you feel internally. Now remove each piece of clothing, naming the shame, and saying aloud, "I remove. . . ." until you are standing naked in front of the mirror. Reflect on how you feel in your body now and what you see.

DEATH

What experiences have you had of death? And how were you taught to navigate them?

Can you see the echoes of this in the smaller losses you experience on a more regular basis and how you deal with them?

Firestarter

How do you picture death? Can you draw a picture of it (does it have a gender for you?) or write a poem about it?

FEMININE DARKNESS AND INITIATION

What initiations have you had into the Feminine darkness? Can you write or tell a story about one or several of them?

How can you create a conscious initiation into the Feminine darkness for yourself?

Firestarters

Possible tools for entering the unconscious include:

> › Burning questions: most spiritual practices, and modern psychoanalysis, use unanswerable questions as cues to internal examination of that which we have not previously examined in order to move us from automatic functioning to conscious examination of our unconscious assumptions.

> › Dreams: these again play a key role in the stories of

all spiritual traditions and modern psychoanalysis as a way of receiving messages from the divine, seeing with greater clarity than in waking life, and understanding previously obscured feelings.

› Automatic writing and intuitive painting are two core ways of facilitating an exploration of the unconscious.

› Active imagination: free association of ideas and words; unplanned speaking in a held witnessed space; continuing the dream state in waking life; lucid dreaming, where the dreamer takes an active part in the dream; trance states, meditations or visualisations which lead us into the unconscious mind.

› Sound, movement or body based work.

› Many therapeutic techniques.

› Hallucinogens.

Each way of encountering the unconscious requires that we move from fear and control to a playful yet serious-minded curiosity. It requires that we find a way of staying safe, whilst taking big adventures into the unknown.

THE WOMB

What is your relationship to your womb? Is it a place of safety or pain? What is coming up as needing healing in this area?

What does your monthly bleeding mean to you?

How is your bleeding connected to your power?

Firestarter

Can you paint or draw your womb as you experience it?

Try creating pieces of art during menstruation and ovulation and comparing them.

6

CLEARING SPACE

One day you finally knew
what you had to do, and began. . .
Mary Oliver, *The Journey*

Bring out your dead
It is time, it is time.
Take your broom in one hand and scythe in the other.
Take your flaming sword and polishing cloth,
Your power hose and pen.
It is time to clear.
Clear your attic, tidy your room,
Sort through the bones, the clutter, the pain,
Sing over them all and watch them take flame.

Our bodies teach us every month that we must clear space before we can gestate life: clearing the old is an integral part of creation. Before we can create the new, before we can increase our power, we must make space.

Do you feel resistance rise up, when I invite you to clear? A little voice that says:

I don't have the time, or energy.
I am scared to lose what is precious to me.

It sounds like hard work.

I've done that already.

Very often as women we are in charge of the cleaning, and usually it is to present a good appearance to others, just as we have been taught to do with our bodies. Superficial tidiness and order are hallmarks of the Good Woman of the patriarchy. We learn to domesticate and disinfect and keep out the wild edges to give the impression that everything is under control. In this model tidiness can be a cover for hidden mess. We bury all that we cannot face under an exterior of apparent calm and order, we stash our unwanted mess behind cupboard doors to avoid shame. This approach can morph into a need for extreme perfection, and become an obsessive illness, as our minds bid to manage everything in our lives which feel out of control, taking all our power and energy. Tidiness here says: *everything's just fine, it is completely under control.* It's what we want the world to believe about us: that order prevails. *Just stay on the surface and don't mess up my cushions.* Because in this model, mess reminds us of the internal chaos that we can't control. Tidying can be a wonderful way to keep ourselves busy and distracted from the real, deep work that needs doing. With the bonus that it gets us praise for being Good Women.

There is another sort of clearing in the patriarchal model. The wholesale clearance that we see in deforestation, rezoning neighbourhoods, the razing of cultures that we see playing out in conquering armies around the world. This says — *everything goes, no ifs, no buts. Something new is coming. We are in charge and what we say goes.* This sort of clearance is cold-hearted and cruel: it imposes a monolithic reality on everyone.

Neither of the above are the type of clearing I am talking about here. It is neither self-destructive, nor destructive of others. It is compassionate and wise. It is both deep and superficial. Its intention is never to cause harm or hurt. It is done in the spirit of the gardener who is looking to strengthen her plants by pruning back the dead wood to make space for new growth. This clearing is a conscious, active engagement with the natural process that is always occurring. Rather than grasping, hoarding, trying to cling on to what has been, it asks us to collaborate in the clearing, so that we can collaborate in the creation that follows.

We must use our strength and focus and take a blade in our own hands and cut back — or transform — everything which is no longer alive or life-giving. We cut back the masculine undergrowth in our life, the old relationship dynamics, the shells of patriarchal mind-sets, the weeds that have self-seeded in our sacred grove, which may have been invisible to our eyes until now. We cut back that which drains us, the inauthentic, the disempowering.

Be brave. The more you cut, the more you can burn.

Feel the fear rise, as you worry that you have done too much already. Cut more. Cut further than you ever dared. Cut your hair. Cut every commitment you have that does not fill you up, that distracts you from your mission. Cut every relationship that drains you. You need to find every briar that grabs your skirt as you walk through the clearing and cut. Every hand that grasps out for you. Or place a clear boundary or limit on that which you cannot cut.

Burning Woman relies on sacred clearing, so that she can see the stark beauty of her own life, unencumbered by assumptions, traditions, expectations, others' stories of her, her own stories of herself. Burning Woman has to be ruthless with great love.

If we do not clear space, then wildfires are more likely to sweep through, when we receive Her presence. Or Her voice, when She calls, may be muffled by the distractions around us, our vision obscured by busyness.

Again and again in your life, Burning Woman, you will be called to prune back this year's growth, to make way for next year's. You will be prompted to take out the dead wood —

old stories, old habits, old dreams and put them to the fire. Through them we can only know ourselves as we were yesterday, they keep us small and trapped. You, Burning Woman, are expansive. You are bigger than those stories.

Do you dare to find out who you are when you burn them all? Do you dare to step into the cauldron of transformation without agenda? Are you prepared to let go of control and burn?

Declutter your house, your mind, your diary. Declutter your obligations. Anything that is not rooted in authenticity. Anything which takes you away from your centre. Anything that demands you be other than who you are must go. Until you find yourself surrounded by space. And still there is more to shed.

Shed your clothes, shed your skins,

Until you are naked.

And seen.

In safe space.

Then you will know what to do.

Then you know who you are.

Then you will feel your own fire.

And in the spaciousness you will hear the call to burn.

CREATING SAFE SPACE

In order to step out of our shells and into our greatness we need a place to be held whilst in the process of transformation. As we step beyond our self-imposed limitations, our learned smallness, inherited inadequacy, our culturally imposed confinement, our trauma and into our power, we need to learn to find—or create—safe space.

A safe space allows you to feel yourself into your own skin. It is one that holds you safely, without judgement, that allows —nay, celebrates—the unfolding of yourself. It is a place to be deeply seen and heard. We cannot transform in healthy ways, when we are caught in a hall of mirrors of trauma, fear and shame. A safe space provides a circle of reflective living mirrors that cheer us into our greatness and witness our full power before we may see it ourselves.

Every woman needs safe space. Yet most of us have experienced few truly safe, held spaces in our lifetimes. For many women it is vital that this space is out of the male gaze. For some it may be important to have a circle of women who know us well, for others a group of strangers is safer.

Dear love, if you don't have one, seek one out, or create a safe harbour for yourself.

Just one. A place where you can be completely yourself. Shamelessly.

And once you have that feeling, you will begin to realise that you deserve nothing less in all your relationships, all the spaces you inhabit. You will begin, in time, to make each and every space you share with others a safe space, for everyone who uses it.

Find or create a space for yourself free from shaming, from shadow power play. One which you are called to step into your authenticity and expect to be received wholeheartedly. You need space which will hold you in your darkness and your light. Which will celebrate your inner burning, and never burn you from without.

You might find this in a red tent, a women's circle, a Facebook group, an art or yoga class, a space in the woods, a therapist's office, your blood sister's lounge or soul sisters' kitchens. You might find it in your clients and co-workers, those who are healing alongside you. You might need several, for various different aspects of your life that you are transforming.

Whilst it is a comfort zone when you need it and a soft place to fall, it must also be a place that will challenge you to be truly authentic to yourself, to your values. It is a place filled with people who will confront you in love and keep you accountable. And importantly it needs to be a space of growth, where not only you, but everyone in it, therapists included, are committed to their own healing and transformation. A safe space is a place to which sometimes you will be drawn, and sometimes you will force yourself to show up and be accountable, when shame and fear are telling you to hide and be small.

A safe space is one that does not demand perfection, but that honours process—it respects the messy, wild chaos of creation, the unformed, the imperfect, the half-baked, everything we have previously been taught to keep silent and hidden. The lie of perfection—which women have been taught and bought— is that if something is not perfect, it is shameful and deserves to be hidden away. In the Feminine, we honour every stage of growth and potential as valid strivings towards a greater wholeness. Safe spaces provide seeding grounds, practice places, playgrounds and workshops for the body and soul as we learn to co-create. We need them to keep us awake, alive, vibrant and healthy.

GOODBYE GOOD GIRL

The question isn't who is going to let me, but who is going to stop me.
Ayn Rand

If I spoke my truth I would be burned
On a pyre of my books.
Fire would rain down.

This is the potential cost of words of fire.
Truth that burns.

Once we have established safe space, and learned the importance of going dark, it is time to shed our inner clothes. Our power hides itself behind habitual masks or personas that we get used to showing to the world.

The way of the Burning Woman asks that we make a bonfire of all our personas, conformity, other people's rules and external authority and mine for the gold of our own authority. It demands that we dig deep into authentic relationship with our own understanding of spirit, ourselves and our soul people and develop an intimate, living, real, reciprocal relationship with all of them.

We each have our own unique personas to unravel, our own masks to sift through and lay down, demote, integrate or throw on the fire.

There are several predominant archetypes of authority that we have internalised and must confront, before we can assume our own sovereignty. The ruling archetypes are different for each of us, based in our life experiences of real life authority figures. Masculine archetypes of authority include: the Shadow Man, the Patriarch—whether Noble King, Absent Ruler or Autocrat, the Drill Sergeant, the Judge, the Critic, the Teacher, the Priest or Guru (whilst these last can of course be either gender, most women I have spoken to report them being masculine figures).

Feminine archetypes of authority are usually dominated by the various "negative" shades of mother: the Stone Mother, the Absent Mother, the Perfect Lady Mother, the Wicked Stepmother, the Devouring Mother. . . Each of these projected by women detached from their own instinctive connection to the Feminine trying to fit themselves into the patriarchal model of the Good Mother.

With and through these stunted authority energies we play

out elaborate dramas in our lives that both captivate and drain us. With each of them we submit ourselves to their authority, judgement, shaming, control or punishment. We live subject to their rules, or in defiance of them, inside our heads, as well as in any versions of them that we come across in our daily lives. In all of these archetypal relationships, we are in the role of the child. We have one of two roles we can play: the Good Girl, always feeding, sharing with, appeasing and healing the authority figure, or the Rebel who rejects and refuses. But both are done in reaction to external authority. Neither are independent, empowered choices: they are responses to an existent power play. Whereas when our energy is freed up from trying to constantly placate them or stop ourselves becoming them, we have a huge amount more power to establish our own sense of self and inner authority.

The Patriarch is he who must be worshipped and obeyed, he who must not be crossed, he who can give favours if we please him. He is omnipresent in all facets of the patriarchy. The Shadow Man is his immature dark side; the King is his light side. Many girls grow up as daddy's little girl, learning to charm and appease the Patriarch to get what they want. They often continue this on with bosses and husbands. When we are trapped in this role of appeasing the Patriarch, we get caught in the traditional feminine role of pleasing, because we believe that he holds all the power.

The various negative Mothers are all crippled by patriarchy; you may recognise your mother as being an example of just one, or of sharing facets of each. The Stone Mother is she who does not respond to our needs, whose body is cold, whose face is unreadable and whose energy is blocked from us. The Stone Mother is she who we long for, but can never have. The Absent Mother is she who is absent — through distraction with lovers, work, travel, sickness or death. Where the Stone Mother is physically present but energetically absent, the Absent Mother leaves a physical void in her daughter's life, which may be made up for with gifts and guilt. The Perfect Lady Mother is she who judges us purely on our external attributes. We are told that we shame her through our dirtiness, uncouthness and vulgarity. She models for us what is required if we are to be proper ladies of the patriarchy: perfect behaviour, no desires of our own, shielded emotions, a focus on appearances and pleasing men. The Devouring Mother is she who believes herself to be powerless, and feeds off the power of others, because her own well-spring is dry. She is cut off from her own source of nourishment, and has embodied the patriarchal myth of the Starving Woman: she dare not feed herself. She is connected to the dark side of the Witch — the dark feminine who gains her life from controlling, enchanting and consuming others.

Bethany Webster in her powerful work on healing the mother wound points out that as daughters we have been taught to be loyal to our mothers, and so a massive and power-draining complex is set up where we dare not become more powerful than our mothers, due to a sense of loyalty. And yet we resent hugely the way they drain us of our energy and hold us back. We resent living our adult lives as Good Girls, trapped in the patriarchal constraints to which we no longer personally subscribe. But to reject them fully, to claim our energy back by calling out the Bad Mother or the Patriarch as fundamentally unhealthy and disempowering, feels like we are risking death. It is perceived as the ultimate treachery, and even as grown-up Good Girls, no longer reliant on their care for our survival, we fear the repercussions of this.

Learning to untangle ourselves from the web of the patriarchy is deeply challenging but essential. If we do not, these primary relationships remain our stunted blueprints for our relationship to the Feminine and with every other person in our lives.

The Good Girl is an aberration of our natural Feminine energy. Our journey into our power happens gradually as we grow up. As toddlers and teens the process intensifies, when we fight to assert ourselves as individuals in the world. But if this process has been thwarted, by family or society, if it seems too dangerous, we step back from the brink and fall into the Good Girl archetype instead.

To take power in our lives, we must give up our role as The Good Girl, dare to question authority, and instate our own in its place. This requires that we revisit the places in our lives when we relinquished our own authority.

The Good Girl learned her lesson well: she knows must submit to survive. Playing the Good Girl convincingly was the closest thing she had to a guarantee of staying safe in the patriarchy — at home and out in the world. She learns not be fully herself for fear of *what if.* Instead she conforms, and looks for the approval of others. She looks outside herself—to parents, peers, and her bible of choice—be it *The Good Book* or *Vogue*—to dictate how she should live, what she should wear, how she should speak, and what is acceptable. The Good Girl learns to put everyone else's needs and desires first, and her own last. She has learned from early on to make herself less: less obtrusive, taking up less space. She has learned to erase her own self. She has been taught to respect the system. And eventually, the Good Girl graduates *cum laude,* fully complicit in her own oppression, as a Good Wife and Mother, ready to raise the next generation of Good Girls.

I know a lot about the Good Girl. She has been me for most of my life. I prided myself on not being a rebel to my parents or teachers. Apart from the occasional mega-whopper tantrum, I did everything within my power to avoid conflict, punishment, rejection. . . I graduated top of my class and carried my lessons out into the world with me. But the more I stepped into my own work, the harder it was for my Good Girl to survive. Each five-star review. Each word of praise for my (dangerous) work prolonged my stay of execution. Each criticism removed my right to express myself, proclaimed me dishonourable.

It was only when I realised that I had been handing my own power to others, because I believed that they had the final say, that they were the arbiters of power, that I understood the truth that had previously evaded me: I had another choice. To keep that power for myself. To approve of myself. Because as an adult woman I got to vote. That power was mine.

I am learning, slowly, to own my own right to exist. To see myself mirrored in those who hold my values. To recognise my own integral power, my own authority. To stop apologizing for myself all the time and stand, wholeheartedly, for myself. But it requires a lot of unlearning. It requires a lot of courage.

I began to see that those who were criticising me, were doing it on their terms, according to their values. . . which we not mine. And I was beginning to do it for them too. Apologising when I didn't fit their view of the world. Judging myself for not doing so, whilst simultaneously trying to live true to myself. I began to find it harder and harder to be in the company of other Good Girls, because I didn't fit in, I wasn't good enough to be a Good Girl. . . and I hated that feeling. By myself or with other Burning Women I felt whole and strong, with the Good Girls I felt naked, stupid, shameful and wrong. And so I was split in myself—trying to be both Burning Woman *and* Good Girl, trying to be silent *and* outspoken. One after the other, or both at once.

But I didn't have the words for it, and neither did they. And so I just felt socially anxious and a bit crazy.

Because the problem with stepping into my own truth, meant simultaneously rejecting theirs. It set up conflict. And as a Good Girl I hate conflict. As a Good Girl I want everyone to like me. But as a Burning Woman I can't stand conformity. And the more I stepped into myself, my own ideas and power, the more painful and alienating this split became: I yearned for approval I could never receive. Because the people I am yearning for it from, are the very ones who cannot give it. They are too invested in the status quo. They are fully signed up to supporting things the way they are. As Burning Women we eventually come to the acceptance that we cannot, will not, receive the approval and celebration of traditional authority figures or conservative friends who are invested in the patriarchy. The sooner we see this and accept it, the easier our lives will be.

As Burning Women we move from our need for external approval in order to stay safe, to moving the locus for approval and decision making within ourselves, as mature adults. We move from the big Father in the sky looking down on us and judging us, and the flawed human mother who could not give what we most needed, to the Great Mother from within holding space for us. We move from obeying and submitting to external power, to co-creating, partnering with the divine, within our Feminine selves.

Letting the Good Girl recede as one of the primary characters in our archetypal selection box is a key part of our initiation as Burning Women. We have to step out of the persona of the Good Girl in order to wear the robes of Burning Woman.

When we do so we fully accept that we will not always be liked, approved of, or applauded as we strike out on our own, and we may well be attacked. But we know that to live our truth is more important to us, than to live their lies for another moment. To live our truth, to be fully connected to life is our reason for being. Then we become the heroines of our own lives, the ones we have been waiting for.

THE HEROINE'S JOURNEY

Whether a woman knows it or not, she is a vessel of great magnitude born capable of reshaping humanity's destiny if she only knew the true depths of her innate gifts.

Be prepared now to see the fierce face of the feminine rock as her inner geographies of volcanic strength erupt from a love she has held in her belly for life all of her days.

This is not a gasp of her last breath. It is her birthing cry into her wise leadership on our planet.

ALisa Starkweather

As we release the archetypal characters that have peopled our personal dramas until now, we must also close the book of stories which we have used to shape our destinations thus far.

The hero's journey has had its time with us: it is time for a new story. We need to make new maps for the new paradigms, new intentions and ways of travelling that we are discovering. We are no longer ersatz heroes, but real heroines on our own sacred journey.

In the heroine's journey we realise that the dragon lies not in a far-off land, but curled within. And so we are called inwards. Into the dark cave of our unconscious.

You creep on tiptoe, into the place you have avoided your whole life, sword in shaking hand, drawing together every wisp of courage to slay this hideous beast that lies coiled on your most precious treasure. You fear his immense power and feel your smallness shaking in your shoes, your skin so soft against his scaly strength. You inch forward until you can smell his sulphurous breath, his muscles ripple as he shifts his sleeping weight, his nostrils beginning to twitch.

Your heartbeat, as loud as a thunderstorm, has registered. He opens his eyes and looks straight at you. You raise your sword. But keep your eyes on his. He opens his mouth to roar. And you do too. You stand your ground and breathing deep into your belly, roar, rather than run and scream. Repeating your claim like a talisman — "This power is mine. I have come to claim it." Repeating it until you, and the dragon, know it for truth.

And suddenly the danger is gone. No fight necessary. That dragon had sat on your power for so long it had come to believe it was its own. You had spent so many years listening to the myths of the dragon, hearing him growl within, you got so scared of these stories, that you never thought to come and meet him for yourself.

The dragon never was your enemy. The treasure never was his. It's yours. It always was. All he was doing was waiting for you to claim it, protecting it from those who would steal or misuse it. He knew his job was to protect it until you were able to care for it as fiercely as he. Until you knew yourself as its rightful owner. Until this great wealth would be used wisely, not to do damage to yourself or others. Until you were learned enough in the ways of the world not to squander it or give it away. That was his sacred role, as your greatest ally and protector.

You can call on him to stand with you any time you need an ally—a visible representation of a powerful guardian to model, support and strengthen you — the fire-breathing dragon: belly full of fire, watchful eyes, scaly impermeable skin, fire spewing from the mouth, committed to protecting what is precious to you.

As women we tend not to be taught to question those who penetrate our power fields. Instead we are brought up to hand over our power, to let others take care of it, and ourselves, in exchange for us taking care of them, emotionally, physically and spiritually. It is a heavy burden, one usually done unconsciously, and yet expected culturally. A woman who is not willing to engage in this exchange is usually shamed as selfish and immature. But it *is* an exchange. So as Burning Women we make a new deal: I take back my power, and I learn to take responsibility for myself. . . and you in return take responsibility for yourself. We may share ourselves and our lives, experience deep love, care, intimacy and connection, but we are each the keeper of our own power. This is the move from co-dependency

—the model engendered by our culture—into independence. Intimacy, penetration and sharing through choice, and consent, not obligation.

*

We may confront many dragons on our path — inner and outer. Each time we must face them, look them in the eye. Each time they roar, we may question their authority clearly with two magic words: *Says who?*

We tend to assume that someone criticising us or limiting us is in a position of authority: we have learned to place others' authority above our own, and tend to do it unquestioningly, unconsciously. Part of taking our power back is moving these unconscious processes into conscious awareness, until we have retrained our instincts. *Says who?* immediately brings conscious inquiry into the power dynamic — be it a shaming internal voice, or one on the outside.

Any thought or comment that arises which makes you stop, shame yourself or make yourself smaller deserves to be carefully examined. Stand there, aware of your own self, your own power, and inquire clearly but assertively—*Says who?*

If a stranger sent you an email demanding that you hand over all your money, or quit your job right now, you wouldn't immediately do it. You would stop and inquire — *who's telling me to do this, what right, what authority do they have?* Pretty much every time you would dismiss their claim to your life, and carry on. But we don't tend to do that in energetic interactions. We tend to forget to stop to check, and just hand over what is being demanded of us: our power, our authority.

Says who? is a simple verbal reminder to yourself of your own dominion over your own power and your need to check the authority and motivation of anyone who lays claim to it, or seeks to disconnect you from your own power.

It works well when we come up against the System too. The System is usually faceless—*Says who?* requires that the System put a face and name to its authoritarian nature so you can look it in the eye. It requires that it states the basis of its authority in words or laws.

We need to learn to consistently challenge the pretenders to our power. In doing so we choose which voices we respond to —internally and externally. We can distinguish the voices which we can trust from those we cannot. Standing in our power, we are ready to hear the call and in answering it, become mistresses of our own destinies.

7

THE CALLING

The Goddess reflects back to us what has been so missing in our culture: positive images of our power, our bodies, our wills, our mothers. To look at the Goddess is to remember ourselves, to imagine ourselves whole.

Kathie Carlson, *In Her Image*

Reclaiming the Feminine is about reclaiming our intuition, the voice that speaks in the dark. About reconnecting with the one who reveals herself in the moonlight, in the whispers of dead leaves crackling under our feet. She, the impermanent One, shining in the eyes of a newborn child and in the creases of an old man's hands. She, the force of change. Powerful beyond measure. Forever untamed. We must accept her in the fullness of her glory, fierce and gentle, soft and wild. Only thus will we be showered with the grace of Her presence.

Nicole Schwab, *The Heart of the Labyrinth*

It is time,
I am here.

For some she came in a dream.
For others in waking life, words as clear as a bell.
She may come in a whisper so loud she can deafen you or a shout so quiet you strain to hear.

She may appear in the waves or the face of the moon, in a red
goddess or a crow.
The voice of She we were told did not exist.
The voice of She we were told not to trust.
The voice of She we did not expect.
Ringing in the darkness,
Calling you home.

Who is She? She is your power, your Feminine source. Big
Mama. The Goddess. The Great Mystery. The web-weaver.
The life force. The first time, the twentieth time you may not
recognise her. Or pretend not to hear. As she fills your body
with ripples of terror and delight.

But when she calls, you will know you've been called. Then it
is up to you to decide if you will answer.

She howls through canyons, claws away insecurities and doubts and
stomps illusions into dust. She rattles hailstones on rooftops and whips
the seas into a froth of fury. She dances the wind into hurricanes
and kindles a wildfire saying, "Watch out it burns. Pay attention!"
She uproots trees with her storming, thunders leaves, branches, and
houses down around your ears crying, "Wake up!" She screeches on
the winds her voice becoming a tornado, swirling madcap down the
corridor of time.
She lifts a chalice of armadillo skin and whale bone and she cries out
for change. In the howl of outrage and sweep of fury, in the crackle
of iced lightning, in the waves which crest against the shore and
drag you out to sea. In the ferocious beauty of her howling dance
we glimpse the sun-heart of love, sharp-edged, ragged, hot slicing
through the veils that shroud our thinking.
We step through and join her dance raising our voices in the chorus
of her song.
Molly Remer

It goes both ways.

She comes when we call too. Whether in despair or delight. She comes when we are lost in the darkness and long for her like water. When we know that we need her.

Don't call her in half-heartedly. Don't commit unless you're sure. Remember she brings great power and creativity, but first she brings burning. And her own agenda and timing. When we call on Burning Woman as our portal to the life force, we announce ourselves willing to turn away from the hero's journey, away from what we have been taught, away from what we have established, and burn.

I say this from experience. The times I have called her in, thinking I was ready, I realised only in retrospect how powerful she was. And quite how unprepared I was, despite thinking that I was strong and ready. Little did I know what answering her invitation would really mean.

We receive many invitations to dance in the fire over our lifetimes, most of the time unexpected, usually inconvenient. Some we accept; other times we decline; sometimes we show up at the wrong address; or when we reach to knock on the door, we think that no one's home, and run back to familiarity.

The invitation into the living came as fire. I was born to the fire sign, and it is the burn that would call me back home. It was terrible and strong and inviting. It came as cancer, as intimacy, as a reckoning with a trauma history that leaves the raised welts of scars against skin and even deeper, inside where arteries mingle with memory. The invitation came and it shook me, it burned me, it branded me as forever awake and aware to the things we try so hard to forget. And so it took me a long time to understand that, though disruptive in its cracked concrete and the terrible want of soft skin, it was a love that was there at its hot centre. It was love that will do whatever it takes, do whatever is required, and do what we think we will not do. It was a love that saved and that healed by keeping me forever marked in the wounding.

It is invitation. And it matters, I think, that I said yes, and walked
through the door without even stopping to pack my bags.
My truth is my love, is my untamed tongue, is my animal instinct
that kept me alive, is my evolution into compassion and radical
defiance. My truth is my fire, is my longing for the firm of her hand
on the small of my back, is my knowing that again and again I
will risk going into the unknown, for where else can I go when the
fire came and shook me awake and nothing could ever be the same
again.

Isabel Abbott

There is nowhere to go. And nothing will ever be the same
again.

Will you answer the call? Will you risk it all?

That is her question.

Burning Woman is the heart and soul of revolution — inner
and outer. She burns for change, she dances in the fire of the
old, all the while visioning and weaving the new.

Where the patriarchy gets hard for tradition and conservatism,
Burning Woman longs for change, as an expression of the life
force, ever-changing and growing. She rejoices in dangerous
acts of creative rebellion which bring forth the spark within
her. She revels in gestures of audacity and daring that thrill and
terrify in equal measure. In these she feels truly alive.

We soon learn that Burning Woman never takes "can't" for
an answer. There is always a way: she will dream it or weave it,
stamp or storm it. She is free from the ties that bind, loosed from
the social constraints that hold us. She calls us to live this way.
She demands that we let go of our Good Girl commitments to
the rules of human mothers and men and instead shows us how
to live by nature's rhythms. She brings wildness to the table and
sets it free in our lives and asks that we stop taking everything
quite so seriously for a moment, and make the space that we
need to take up in our fullness.

She sets her terms, her RSVP: if we commit to show up and play with her, again and again and again. If we commit to getting naked, vulnerable and intimate with her. If we stop holding ourselves back and controlling every step of the way, then she will use her dark mirror to reflect back our greatness.

Trust the urge to burn, she whispers by way of invitation, *and let it guide you.*

The yearn to burn gives you wings to fly. It is rocket fuel that takes you to the moon and back and lets you stay up all night. She is the Firestarter, the spark to dry wood, the breath that builds the flames.

Hers is the delight in setting fire to things and watching the blaze, the sheer abandon, the hedonistic rush of letting go, of facing our smallness and blowing it sky high.

Hers is the voice that burns bright and clear, taking you by the roots of your hair, shaking the mud from your ears as you try to ignore her calls.

The Muse is she who burns,
The Goddess is she who burns,
Your desire is she who burns. . .
She flows like honey, slithers like a snake,
Presses her groin into yours and looks you straight in the eye.
She carries the whiff of danger, like jasmine, between her thighs,
And promises you a brave new world of delights. . .
If you will burn the known world first.
Dare you burn everything you love and hold dear?
Will you hold it up to the fire and watch what burns and stays?
Will you test the strength of the love you profess, the art you
cherish, the connection you believe in?
Will you baptise all you hold dear in the flames?
Dare you see your own soul?

BAPTISMS OF FIRE

In the high plains of the Andes, they say that if you are struck by a bolt of lightning, it is a sign. It is the mark of the shaman, the one who is blessed with fire and survives. The one who has befriended the Great Spirit and can henceforth serve as a bridge between the seen and the unseen.
Nicole Schwab, *The Heart of the Labyrinth*

You must be ready to burn yourself in your own flame. How could you become new if you had not first become ashes?
Nietzsche, *Thus Spake Zarathustra*

For many Burning Women, the initiation to Feminine power comes in a baptism of fire: a bolt from the blue, which burns to the ground their previous identities whether they are ready or not. For some it has come in the form of serious, debilitating illness, for others it has been the death of a loved-one, a public burning of shame, heartbreak, disaster at work, a car crash, a major parenting issue, the literal burning down of their home, an acrimonious divorce, loss of career, financial disaster or often several of these compounded within a short period, leaving the woman reeling, her previous identity in ashes. Women often describe these experiences in terms of natural disaster — a wildfire, tornado or storm tearing through their lives.

The defining factors of a baptism of fire are that we feel overwhelmed or destroyed by forces completely outside of our control. Because we have not consciously initiated the transformation process, or not in the severity with which it happens, the degree of shock and trauma can be massive. Weeks, months or even years can be lost in the resulting liminal state as we wander in the underworld. We may feel that we have been burned alive, gutted and when the experience is over, we cannot believe we are still here. Much of what we loved, identified with or devoted ourselves to is gone. We feel the aching pain of the hole it has left in us. We find ourselves looking into the chasm, not knowing how to continue now that a major part of our self-definition has been taken from us and can never be restored.

We have to learn who we are without this known identity. And then somewhere, in the heart of our darkest despair and excruciating grief, we realise that we are braver, stronger, more whole than we ever thought possible. In the depths of our suffering, we see the seeds of our deepest potential.

This is the destructive power of the Feminine. This is Burning Woman claiming you for her own. Usually after you have ignored her calls, refused her invitations and decided to go your own merry way. You can turn your back, cower, hide and feel angry or victimised and be broken down by the experience. Or you can surrender to her, break open, switch power sources and learn to harness this power.

My baptism of fire happened in a series of waves.

In the first wave, over the course of six weeks I had been attacked or confronted and run from and shut down to more semi-strangers than I ever had in my life. It was as though every path I turned down was inhabited another woman set on misunderstanding me and baying for my blood. It was extraordinary the intensity of chaos that seemed to spiral around me attracting discord. For a Good Girl it felt like death.

What makes me laugh ruefully now is that I brought it on myself. As I stood on the beach on my thirty-fourth birthday and called out to the sea — *Bring it on. I'm ready.*

So she did. Oh mama, she did.

A hectic few months preceded it. I had recently started getting braver writing about and teaching about things I previously hadn't had the courage to do. Namely sex and women's power. I was feeling very exposed. Contributing to a couple of large events, doing author interviews and totally redesigning my blog, leading to multiple panic attacks about being seen. I was just about to start Womancraft Publishing with my husband and knowing that we were going to be entirely self-employed which meant massive financial instability for the foreseeable future with a young family in tow.

My immune system was knocked out by nine weeks of illness: a tooth infection, flu, ear infection, tonsillitis... and the three courses of powerful antibiotics I had been given to treat them. Medication has a tendency to spark anxiety and depressive episodes in me. I couldn't work... and my husband's hours were cut in half. Adrenal fatigue brought me to my knees.

And then, just as I tried to lay down more of my commitments so that I could get better, a woman I was working with lashed out at me using words that cut me to the core. I was knocked for six. It was a complete bolt from the blue. This was a project that I had poured my heart and soul into, which was destroyed in a matter of moments, and with it my trust: *who could I trust and who was against me?* I had no way of knowing. A sacred women's circle lay in tatters and I felt naked and terrified.

I began physically shaking. Suicidal and self-harm thoughts racing. Panic attacks rained down on me. Her words running on a loop through my head. If what she said was true. If lots of people thought it, then my work was a sham. The trust we had built was a sham. And if I did so much harm when I was trying to do good, then my self-judgement was obviously way off whack.

I was being boiled alive in a thick vat of sticky shame.

And so I did what I know. I ran and hid. I stepped away from everything. And cried and shook and hid.

My husband held me and rocked me like a baby as I sobbed, and tried to disentangle her words from my own truth.

But I couldn't. I couldn't find where in myself those words did not define me. They obliterated everything I had known about myself, and left me dark and scared and alone.

Every night for a week I was murdered in my dreams, over and over — stabbed, shot, chased, ripped to shreds. Night after night I would have to wake myself up and breathe through the shaking and keep myself awake until the dream had passed over.

This was followed by more run-ins with women I barely knew who smelled blood. I left more and more groups, cut more ties, trying to find somewhere safe, anyone safe.

And then, just as the dust was starting to settle, and my body was beginning to stop shaking, in the midst of the launch of our business's first two books, I crashed my father's car, writing it off. I had been the way to the airport to go to a "How to Make Money" conference. I kid you not. The brand new car I crashed into was covered under our insurance, but the one I was driving was not. And so the first bit of money we had earned from our fledgling business went up in flames too. And I shook, and shook, and shook.

This was what I now recognise as a baptism of fire. No one ever taught me how to recognise one before. Or how to move through one. When I didn't feel like I was dead or dying or engulfed in blackness, I had an intuitive sense that it was a time of transformation — writings from the time centre on the darkness, shaking and metamorphosis. But it felt so lonely. So very, very personal. But in it I found my real allies, those who could hold space for me, hold me, listen to me, and share their own stories of burning.

I didn't know the process at first, and so I moved through slowly, very painfully, on every level — physical, emotional, spiritual. I suffered thorough it, struggled with it. I took it personally. I longed to be dead or done with it. But the longer I have lived, the more women I have witnessed go through it, the fear of the personal side of it diminishes a little. I have learned a deep respect for the process itself, and rather than constantly trying to force it in order to get to the other side, as we are taught in the patriarchal model, I am learning and re-learning that it is the process itself, not the end result, which is life's deepest gift to us.

It is hard to feel the blessing of a baptism of fire at the time. We can often feel ourselves victims of it. If we subscribe to the belief that we deserve good things, the universe is a friendly place, we are in control, people should be nice or any other of the things we are taught to believe, then we can feel victimised, as though *these bad things are happening just to us, and it's not fair.* Victimhood is what women and others have been taught for generations —we need to get out of this as fast as possible. It will keep us in the darkness for far longer than we need to be there. This is different to shutting down our feelings, or numbing ourselves with fake optimism. We must feel our feelings and keep moving through them. It is vital not to deny their reality. But we need to relinquish the mantel of personal honour for our suffering.

What I have come to see, from the women who have shared their stories with me since, is that it is not personal. The baptism of fire is a universal experience for women moving into their power and out into the world. The darkness is part of the process. The baptism of fire is part of the process. They cannot be avoided. They are necessary, essential parts of transition which enable the radical leaving behind of old selves that is required to move forward into greater power.

THE POWER PROCESS

Fire transform me.

Bring me to my passion!

I choose life. Yes! I choose courage.

To dance among the flames.
ALisa Starkweather, *Daughter of the Earth* CD

Burning woman, you have not been shown how to burn.

Nor taught how the process works.

You see your otherness as failure. As shame.

But your burning is your gift to the world.

The journey from the feminine to the mature Feminine is a process that the female body and soul are innately programmed for and continue to attempt, despite the lack of support or understanding for it in the mainstream of our current culture. Each stage of our biological changing seems to herald a corresponding inner shift. Each physical change opens up a potential portal for transformation, away from older identities and towards new ones. It is as though Burning Woman is the archetypal Feminine we all have within us from birth, one we are programmed to be, and our role is to unwrap ourselves, at each birthday and each rite of passage, to come closer and closer to our power.

Our journeys of transformation tend to be marked by passing through portals of real blood and spiritual fire. They are journeys both of the inner and the outer body. These are rarely discussed or depicted, and so the journey can feel even more terrifying, than in cultures where these rites of passage are taught, celebrated and guided.

These portals of transformation can happen at any time, but there are key times in our biological and spiritual growth where they tend to occur. They also happen on a more frequent basis during the menstrual cycle at the energetic peaks of ovulation and pre-menstrual phase, post-coitally and during profound spiritual experiences. At these times we are in direct contact with our power.

Key elements of our passages of transformation tend to include:

› A raised temperature — the burning.

› Raised or greatly lowered libido.

› Stormy moods and big feelings.

› Blood or mucus.

› Physical and emotional shakiness and trembling.

› Visions or powerful dreams.

These let us know that turbulence is approaching and the storm winds of change are blowing our way. Our bodies pick up their signals early on if we know how to look.

› Your sense of self begins to feel shaky and tenuous.

› Your body feels like it has a life of its own.

› You may feel like you are swinging between being two people, or have totally lost your identity.

› Feeling slightly out of body.

› A sense of resistance or wanting to run. . . or to dive in, speed up or intensify the process.

These "symptoms" can be particularly troubling for those of us who like to feel strong and in charge. In the masculine paradigm of power what is valued is strong-mindedness; calm emotional states; clear-headedness; strong, still bodies and consistency. Whereas when the Feminine power breaks through, shakiness is its handmaiden: a shaky voice, feeling wobbly, lack of clarity in our thoughts, physical tremors. Shakiness is a core symptom of transformation. It does not need to be stopped or controlled, we do not need to shame ourselves or understand it rationally. When we are shaking we need to hold space for ourselves, we need to reach out and ask trusted others to hold us, physically or energetically, as we settle into awareness of our energy and bodies, neither forcing ourselves forward, nor holding ourselves back, simply being in this state and trusting the process.

At these power points, rite of passage rituals or initiations are extremely helpful, giving us strength, support, resources, space and acknowledgement for our journeys from the known to the unknown. They help us to stay grounded in our bodies, bringing our mental and physical energy to the process. They encourage us to discard old habits and belongings that are no longer needed and provide a network of support and witnessing.

If we are lucky enough to feel anger or grief during this time, these emotions give us the energetic impetus that can help us burn through faster. Put your focus on allowing the feelings to flow through you as much as you can — by talking, by writing, by moving, by crying, yelling or screaming — whatever it takes to allow the energy to move through your body. You are a channel for this immense power.

The fear at this stage always is that this is how it will be forever. It will not. Things will change. Not back to how they were, but they will change. Allow others to hold space for you, to care for you, as you wander the Earth in your crazy grief, your rawness, your fury and desolation. At times like this it feels like you are walking around without a skin — and you are —your old shell has cracked open—you are more vulnerable to infection, overwhelm and exhaustion.

We need to understand the process of transformation intimately to be able to move through it more consciously and allow it to flow and unfold rather than block or control it.

The process of embodying Feminine power has a distinct pattern and structure that our bodies instinctively know. It is not the pyramid of masculine power, but the endless flowing of the spiral. It will lead you in and out of the darkness and towards the fire. This spiral journey of transformation is the natural process of growth in all things.

As Burning Women we seem called to embody the process more frequently and acutely. I have watched her in process, read her tale in blog posts, articles and books enough times to see the pattern. You will recognise that this book takes this form, more or less, leading you through the process as you map it onto your own life. You will notice the regular flips between darkness and light, expansion and contraction, creation and destruction, togetherness and solitude. This is the process that Burning Woman commits to living again and again. The order may be a little different, the process may stall, or go in mini loops... your entry point may not be at the threshold but midway along. Some parts may go on for months or even years, others may pass in a matter of hours. But the process is the process.

The Threshold

We have an intuitive sense, an inkling, that things are about to change, that something is coming.

The Calling/Invitation

This may come as an internal prompting: a dream, a vision, a phrase sounded once or repeated. It may be an external voice or job calling us to power. It may be a calling spotted in a flurry of synchronicities. If heeded and stepped into, the process goes faster, if resisted, denied or ignored the process becomes more intense.

Baptism of Fire

The point of physical initiation with power. It often takes the form of a death, illness, disaster, accident or a number of stressful events, each compounding the previous. This **Portal of Transformation** either takes us **direct to the fire circle**... or **down into the darkness**. Either way it is often accompanied by shaking — with nervousness, anxiety, fear, excitement, exhilaration. At this point the shadow power can emerge fully-fledged and trauma symptoms may return.

The Clearing

This may be conscious or unconscious. . . or both. The question is: will we do it, or will it be done to us?

The Darkness

This is your time in the underworld, the shadowlands, No Man's Land where you will be guided by intuition. It provides the necessary emptiness for inner growth — like a cocoon holding a caterpillar as it transforms into a butterfly. It may be a deeply peaceful time, or one filled with angst and terror.

Stepping into the Fire Circle

This is the second **Portal of Transformation**. Again shaking happens. This is the birthing process, our breaking out of our cocoons, stepping out of the darkness and up to the fire once more. It requires renewed energy, vision, courage and purpose.

Dancing Naked Around the Fire

From our cocooned aloneness, we re-join our community. We bring our power out into the world as an active principle and are witnessed as we share our gifts authentically. This is a time for celebration and thanksgiving.

The Ashes

Dancing around the fire always has repercussions as we share our inner experiences with the world. We may experience praise, shame, a vulnerability hangover. . . Shadow power may emerge in ourselves or others looking for resolution. We may experience burnout if we do not commit to profound self-care, or full integration and healing.

This brings us back to **the darkness**, and the circle turns once more.

8

ADVENTURES IN ENERGY ALCHEMY

There is energy released from within that carries with it the power to heal. First destruction, then creation... The fire burns through the old structures eradicating them, transmuting their energies to a higher vibrational level. Then the creative energy released from the destruction allows for the cure of whatever ails the body.

Vicki Noble, *Shakti Woman*

Burning Woman is one who learns how to consciously work with her own biological energy, as well as the spiritual energy that pours though her and the wider elemental energies around her in order to re-weave reality. She is serving a life-long apprenticeship to learn how to:

› Stimulate energy.

› Store energy.

› Ground energy.

› Transmute energy from one form to another.

› Give out energy.

› Receive energy.

› Recharge and conserve energy.

As Burning Women we are embodied energy alchemists, conscious conductors of Feminine energy to the planet, and healers of imbalance for ourselves, our communities and those we work with. We are learning to run ever stronger currents through our systems, until eventually we, and our Feminine power source, are inseparable. This requires awareness, familiarity with the process, learning how to ground and contain energies. It takes practice. And requires exquisite self-care as standard.

Once we accept her invitation, we are always being beckoned to step up closer to the fire and channel forth more energy: to do this we must heal more within us. The process can be arduous, the healing can be hard, and the journey is endless. We can stall or block. . . or we can stay in flow with the process to power, which transforms us in every way as it works through us.

A core function of Burning Woman is to take back her own energy — creative, spiritual, sexual, political and commit to her own self-definition, in order to more fully and authentically gift her unique offerings to the world. She dedicates herself to being the mistress of her own power.

Western science is still in its infancy of really understanding the energy in our bodies and how consciousness works, and so the subject is considered fringe or esoteric. In our culture working with bio-energy is completely overlooked except in alternative or holistic circles. But this energy is the bedrock of our beings, the foundation of our thoughts, feelings and actions. It is life force in pure form, before it is made into matter. And it is constantly being impacted by people and objects and environmental factors around us, beneath our level of conscious awareness.

For women, the emotional body and its energetic field are central to our health, but our medical system has no understanding of them or way of cultivating health in them. Rather they focus on the only thing that they some comprehension of: the physical body, and often their methods of "healing" cause greater trauma and imbalance in the rest of the body.

The Burning Woman needs to find and develop practices to support her energy body. She learns to build her power in her lower chakras. These are the colours of fire: the lowest is red, centred around the anus, adrenals and base of the spine, and connected to feeling rooted and belonging. The next, located in the genitals and womb, is coloured orange and is connected to our sexuality, creativity and feminine power. The third is our solar plexus, our masculine power centre, our will to act and is coloured yellow.

In healthy development the energy passes through each of these during our childhood, each one awakening in a natural sequence. However, many Burning Women will have experienced blockages or freezing in the energy at key points in their development. In order for the life force energy or kundalini to climb up through these centres of power, they need to be open. Otherwise they block the energy and it becomes stagnant.

At an energetic level, this is the process of Burning Woman — strengthening and gaining conscious control of these key chakras, so that the kundalini energy of Burning Woman can rise up through them.

This feminine fire is a primordial, elemental force that is powerful beyond our wildest imaginings. It is, in fact, power itself.
Teri Degler

We need strong containers for the energy to pass through — otherwise it simply leaks out and dissipates. If our own biological energy levels are low, we are frazzled by it. If we cannot contain and focus it, it burns through us and burns us out. So strengthening our bodies, especially our core muscles of the psoas, pelvic floor, lower back is key to our health. As is learning ways to allow this energy to pass through us.

Many systems have developed methods to work with the energetic body, impacting what we take in, and what we emit. They have developed ways of creating energetic shields or boundaries, to prevent unwanted energies from entering our bodies, for cleansing the body of unwanted energies and for emitting clear frequencies.

However, because this field is outside of Systemic control it is all considered deeply suspect. There are many practitioners in all disciplines who have real, practical understanding and ability to work with these energies — from craniosacral workers and reiki practitioners, to psychics, shamans, witches, body workers and constellation therapists, but there are also many whose abilities are not what they would lead gullible people to believe and who make dangerous or naive, ego-based claims. Seek healing, and tread carefully.

Find ways, dear love, of staying open, but safe.

Held in your vulnerability.

As you nurture your connection to source.

As you embody the power of Burning Woman.

WOMEN IN POWER — HARNESSING NEW ENERGY SOURCES

You think I'm not a goddess?
Try me.
This is a torch song.
Touch me and you'll burn.
Margaret Atwood

As Burning Women we are working in the dark, with energies and concepts that have been hidden, which we still do not have full conceptual frameworks for. We are working on the growing edge of what humanity knows to be possible, learning the answers by trial and error as to what comes next. What comes after the healthcare, spiritual traditions, economics, work and family structures that we know now? It can feel lonely. Scary. Because most people are still fully invested in inhabiting and defending the old structures of power, they are unquestioningly running on the old established power sources: financial wealth, fossil fuels, prestigious jobs, caffeine, prescription drugs. . .

Burning Woman is moving beyond these. Perhaps led by her ideology, or her dreams of something better. Perhaps from an experience of seeing behind the curtain of power, and recognizing the sham that it is. Perhaps through being hurt or abused by the patriarchy. Or her body and soul may have said in clear terms that it is no longer possible or sustainable for her to run in the way that is expected of her in 'normal life', through illness which the System has no answers for.

Burning Woman is learning, discovering, co-creating new ways of living for herself on the fly. Her life is the testing ground. She is her own experiment. She is having to reinvent the wheel — how she earns her money and how much she needs, how she cares for her health, her definition of work, family and success. She gets it 'right' for herself. . . and may be misunderstood, judged, condemned. She gets it 'wrong' and may feel despondent, frustrated or ashamed. Again and again, she experiences herself as fallible and human as she lives into new ways of being that she has only the haziest sense of, but an instinctual trust in.

This is challenging in a culture which expects solid business plans, rational, logical explanations and perfection. Our culture is harder still on women who show human fallibility. We are taught in a hundred different ways that as a woman you must not step out in your power unless you are perfect and beyond reproach, and unless you please all the people all the time.

But our bodies are showing us what our minds refuse to believe: this world is burning us all alive.

Just as we women are stepping into power, many of us are having to step back as our bodies collapse. Our spirits may be willing, but our bodies just aren't able to function in this way.

We were not made to run on minimal sleep, high stress, caffeine loaded, calorie controlled diets, all day, every day of the week as modern women do. We cannot live middle-class life styles on ever-diminishing and unreliable incomes. We cannot work full days and be loving mothers and partners and housewives.

The message of inflammation, of adrenal fatigue and autoimmune disease — all which are on the rise in epidemic proportions, especially amongst women — is something that my next book *Medicine Woman*, explores in more detail. Our bodies are registering danger: *step back,* they warn us through myriad disabling symptoms *this is not sustainable.*

Our bodies are asking us to look again at how we live our values, and where we source our energy from.

If we are to be women in power, then it must be power on very different terms to the patriarchal model we were raised in. We have to find a new source of energy. New structures of power. Ones that don't deplete us or our environment.

We have two options: to suffer in silence, or to find new ways forward to transmute the pain into learning. We have to change, and change now. Even if we don't have the answers. Even if we "fail" many times as we try.

Our bodies are calling us to reclaim our power. Calling us into caring enough for ourselves, for the world around us, to dare to be different, to place our own lives in the crucible of transformation, to risk shame and fear, to make mistakes, so that we can find a new way forward: one that is healthy for us all.

Enough already, our bodies call.

Get me back to my native habitat.

To air that doesn't burn and passion that does.

To food that heals and time that unfolds kaleidoscopically,

Weaving millennia together rather than

Chopping us off and ticking away on a second hand.

Enough second-hand living.

I long to live all in. Live real.

Join me! Step out of man-made time

And into your woman cycle.

RECLAIMING OUR POWER

For a woman to actually repossess herself and to centre there is a monumental task, taking years of difficult, painstaking work. . . Once a woman has done the work of re-membering herself, she is much more able to change the world effectively.
Vicki Noble, *Shakti Woman*

The first time I embodied my full Feminine power was on all fours of the sitting room floor. . . as I roared out my first child. The very thing I feared might destroy me, actually most empowered me. I remember the feeling as each part of my body opened and released, allowing the massive surges of energy to spread through my physical self as I birthed my child.

I have felt this power pulse through me as I stood on the beach looking out to sea on a windy day, feeling totally alive, and as I stood back from a painting which had just emerged from my brush. I have felt it as my husband and I came to powerful shuddering orgasms together. I have felt it as I stood in a crowd of several hundred thousand people in the centre of London, marching for peace. Though the circumstances were all very different, the experience is the same: a felt sense of the dynamic electricity of the life force itself pulsing through me at full voltage. It combines authentic self-expression, mixed with a complete falling away of self to incorporate a bigger power. It is a moment when you feel completely yourself... and yet larger than yourself. You feel like a hundred-foot statue of flesh and blood. You are engaged with a greater strength beyond you and can feel pulsations of energy emitting from you. You are completely connected to yourself, your own power, and your power source, to all those around you, and that which you are directing the energy towards.

When we switch our allegiance to the deep Feminine as our source of power, the deep tap root of Feminine energy and support that is our birth right, it requires changing power sources. Just like adapting a car from petrol to electric, or a house from being on the main electrical grid to off-grid, it tends not to be a simple, one-time fix. However, once we show up willingly and we make self-care and deep inquiry a regular habit, something shifts to help us, changes compound further changes—a natural unfolding, disintegration, and reintegration take on a life of their own.

The deep Feminine, the mystery of consciousness, she who is life, is longing for our transformation as much as we are. She holds back, allowing us free reign to choose, nudging us occasionally with synchronicities, illness, births and deaths... But when we make space for her, she rushes into all the gaps, engulfing us with her desire for life and expression. This is what she longs for, this is what we are for: experiencing life at full force through ourselves.

Once we start to work with Feminine power we begin to see that it is not our minds that are in control of this power

— it ebbs and flows with the movements of the planets, the procession of the seasons, the moons and tides, our own internal cycles of menstruality, anniversaries, the events around us. All these and more impact our experience and expressions of power. We learn to become aware of these various energies and their impact on us and work more consciously with, rather than against or in spite of, them. We learn that they are all part of the same process. We open towards the energy, rather than shut down to it. We learn to trust the flow, rather than snatch and grab, hoard and hide. We learn to trust *enough*.

As women stepping into our power we need to become exquisitely aware of the charge in our bodies — when they are becoming depleted, and when they are being augmented. When we are connected, and when we are not. We become attuned to the feeling of being centred, and knowing when we have been knocked off our centres into old energy patterns of defence or grasping. We need to be aware that each step we take into our power, requires that we acclimatise to this experience of greater charge and openness, it requires that we increase our self-care practices, put in place systems to support every area of our life. We need to do this time and again on the spiral path.

We have been disconnected from ourselves, from our power, from each other and the world on so many levels in what Charles Eisenstein calls "The Story of Separation", that we need to work on many levels simultaneously to reconnect to our sources of power: our spirituality, our bodies, the Earth, our lovers, other women, the language we use, the way we work, our relationship to money. We reconnect to our feelings, our hearts, guts, wombs, to our creativity and anger. And as we do this we begin to see that we are all touched through each other's individual healing. None of us are islands, and each act we make inspires, influences or impacts many others.

GROUNDING OUR POWER

When you feel the need to speed up, slow down.
African Proverb

A Burning Woman needs to run on her energy supplies sustainably. This is not as easy as it seems, both because the need for speed has been ingrained into her by the patriarchal model outside, and her own nature. Burning Woman tends to be impetuous and impatient—she can feel the fire inside and longs to burn now. She longs to discharge the divine discomfort and rest in ecstatic bliss.

The need to get this fire out is half pain, half pleasure, like fire ants crawling round inside her skin. Her need to create, to speak, to act is all-consuming—she feels that she must burn now, or die from the intensity of the flames within. But living the fire cycle at this constant pace exhausts the physical body. Without consciously going dark, burnout is only around the corner. How can we learn to temper the fire? How can we find ways to answer its call, whilst caring deeply for ourselves? How can we unlearn the habits of a lifetime of burning ourselves alive for the benefit of others? How can we begin to disengage from the archetype of the martyr? How to moderate the burning without putting it out?

We have not had the grounded woman modelled to us — instead we have seen the disempowered woman, the martyred woman, the sick woman, the starving woman and the burned out woman. We see the woman racing around as though electrocuted and then collapsing in a pile of ash.

We as women have been taught, in a rather second-hand manner, how to run on a minimal, domestic supply of energy. But when we step into our Feminine power, into direct connection with the Source power, we need to be able to contain and express it in its raw, fiery fullness. As Burning

Women we need to be aware of the strength of the energies that we are working with, and learn how they function, otherwise they can knock us out.

All electrical power supplies must be grounded, so that in case of overspill or accident, the flow of energy will disperse into the ground — to which they are naturally drawn. So it is with the power that Burning Women are tapped into. We need to learn to ground the energy that comes through us, so that it doesn't destroy us in the process.

Grounding is the act of strengthening the feeling of being inside the body and connected to the ground or Earth. It is a powerful tool for healing trauma and distributing excess current running through our bodies that can induce anxiety, panic, hyperactivity, mania, all of which lead to further exhaustion of our systems. I have learned this firsthand, the hard way.

Burning Women find their own practices to suit their bodies and temperaments best, from meditation to yoga, deep breathing to dance, running to tai chi, kickboxing to cold water swimming. We need to find ways to release the energy within our bodies and allow room for the new supplies always pouring in.

When we step out in service, when we begin to create, teach, lead and rebel on a bigger scale, we also need to establish practices that can help us to stay connected to our Source power. If we try doing it on our own domestic supply, we will soon burn out. Just like expecting a powerful machine to run by itself without an energy supply, we cannot run at full capacity without maintaining a direct functioning and well-grounded connection to our energy source.

TRAUMA AND ENERGY BLOCKAGE

Enduring internal tension creates heat that ignites alchemical transformation. When we engage mindfully with the practice of holding the opposites we are physically strengthening the container of our body.
Eila Kundrie Carrico, *The Other Side of the River*

In every moment we have two possible responses: to open or to shut down to the energy passing through us. Faced with fear of the unknown, worrying about shame or judgement, experiencing a lack of safety or love, most minds and bodies shut down. And the flow of the emotional experience is blocked.

Trauma is what happens when our bodies contract in fear during a major experience. Trauma is the stifled scream, the frozen body, racing heart, white knuckles, the resistance with every fibre of our beings to the energetic experience unfolding around us.

When we think of trauma we tend to associate it with major events—a car crash, a serious loss or injury. But there are many others including the constant grind of low level, accumulated stress and ill health; childhood trauma which has not properly healed and genetically inherited trauma. As the daughters of patriarchy, many of us have lived in trauma as our default our whole lives.

The key to trauma is not, according to stress expert Irene Lyon, the severity of the event, but how the nervous system responds to it. Significant stresses in your life beforehand can make what initially seems a small event overwhelming to our systems, as they are already running at capacity. Trauma moves our systems into adrenalin-overdrive, disconnection from ourselves, our bodies, other people and our power.

If an intense experience —fear, anger, helplessness or shame —is blocked or repressed, rather than felt and released, then each time our systems experience an overload of energy — whatever the circumstances — in the place we associate with it, our bodies remember. The energy that was experienced at that time, which was trapped in the body, becomes reactivated and we relive the event, physically, mentally and emotionally.

This is why many Burning Women become ill, exhausted, anxious, depressed or traumatised through their early interactions with Feminine power. Stepping into the fullness of our power activates the parts that have been frozen in time through trauma, showing us the parts of ourselves that are in need of healing, before we can safely carry extra charge.

Energy doesn't stay vital for long. As any engineer will tell you, storing power is the hardest thing — it needs to be used or it begins to dissipate. But in the body, denser, more 'negatively' hued energies tend to solidify — as muscle tension, body armouring or mental blocks. And so we need to find ways to access and release these energetic blocks. But our instinctive response, when we are in a state of fear, is that of self-protection or self-defence. So when we hit an area of damage, tension, scarring, we instinctively move away from this point of pain, to avoid the suffering and intensity we know is stored there.

Traumatised individuals tend to go into numbing patterns using repetitive actions which work as self-soothers in order to return to normality. Mine over the years have included: TV, chocolate, alcohol, cake and carbs, work, books and the internet (especially social media) — each gives a hit of endorphins and a sedative effect, to dampen down anxiety when it gets to unmanageable levels. Others self-medicate with drugs or painkillers, with excessive tidying or cleaning rituals. All these act to distract our minds and bodies from the intensity of feeling which we believe we cannot handle. In order to heal, we must find another way: a way to feel, process and finally release that which has been blocked within us.

TRANSMUTING PAIN

Give it to the fire.

It's time to let it go.

Give it to the fire.

Believe that it is so.

Give it to the fire.

No need in hanging on.

Give it to the fire. Release and it is gone.

Give it to the fire. Transform. Give it to the fire. Transform.
ALisa Starkweather

The trauma and fear we experience is not just our own, it has been passed down the generations to us. The current war on terrorism, hot on the heels of two deeply traumatic world wars, not to mention countless civil wars, has ensured that pretty much every human on the planet, over the course over more than a hundred years has been consistently exposed to terror and trauma on a daily basis, either personally or through media coverage. This is before we consider the birthing, parenting, medical and schooling practices which have made the fight, flight or freeze defence mode of existence standard. Living under this level of threat — on a global and personal level has stopped creativity, stopped burning questions and valid challenges to impotent hegemony. It has cryogenically trapped our culture. It is time to transmute this trauma and pain —not just for ourselves, but for those who came before and those who will come after.

We have each developed our own personal ways of responding to energies that we find threatening — these are known as defence structures. First formulated by Wilhelm Reich and Alexander Lowen and later developed therapeutically by

Barbara Ann Brennan, they are ways of understanding how we respond to the world and our interactions with other people. I will outline them here, as they are an important piece of the puzzle, and recommend that you explore them further.

Each structure was created at a specific point in our development, when we sensed that the world around us was not safe, and that we needed to defend ourselves from it. The first to develop is the schizoid response, in those of us who felt rejected in some way from birth. We don't like being here and often escape energetically through just spacing out. The oral character develops in response to feeling abandoned or not getting enough whilst we are still dependent on others, so we are always trying to get more from others to fill us up. The psychopathic defence develops later in childhood and reflects a belief that aggression is the only way to get what we want, whereas the masochistic defence is developed in response to a domineering parent who doles out conditional love based on guilt and shame, and so we learn to withhold our love, and ourselves, from others. The final defence, the rigid structure, develops after early creative rejection, we learn to suppress our emotions and feelings to provide an unruffled exterior.

What started out as an important method of self-defence by a small instinctive and vulnerable child, has now hardened into a habitual way of interacting. In order to open into bigger, braver more power-full versions of ourselves, our out-worn defence structures must crack and fall, to be replaced with consciously created boundaries. I love Matt Licata's call to action on this:

When your emotional world is on fire and you are burning for resolution. . . pause, touch the earth, and slow way, way down. Set aside the demand for relief, for just a moment, and cut into the hardwired sense of urgency. Something is emerging out of the unseen, dark rich soil of the body, longing to come back into the vastness. See clearly whether it must be shifted, transformed, or healed. . . for now.

Depending on the unique configuration of your early history —and the specific nature of the relational field around you —you learned to care for yourself by employing one of two strategies. In the face of surging vulnerabilities, you learned to deny, repress, or shut down — or, to react quickly to resolve the burning, scrambling and spinning out toward the world and toward others to regulate the intensity for you.

While it may be tempting to pathologize these early strategies, seen with eyes wide open, they are revealed to have been intelligent, creative, and necessary at the time, to prevent overwhelm and disintegration in the tender brain and raw nervous system of a sensitive little one, who was utterly dependent on the holding field of others.

But here you are now. It is 10, 20, 30, 40 years later — and the same feelings, emotions, and sensations are erupting. The neural pathways of repression and relief are alive and well. The fragrances of fight/flight/freeze are inviting you into the old grooves of denial and acting out. The long-lost pieces and the orphaned vulnerabilities are still looking for you, yearning to be allowed back home into spacious being.

And you are here. Now. With capacities you once did not have. With awareness, with compassion, and with loving presence, you can rewire the pattern of self-abandonment with the radical groove of presence, of self-care, and of kindness. You no longer need to abandon yourself with the ancient strategies of repression and relief, but to update your holy nervous system with the commitment to staying close, to practicing intimacy, and to the sacred process of metabolization by love.

But please remember that this new groove is of the unknown, it is unprecedented, and will take practice to implement. It is the neural channel of love, emerging out of the unseen to reorganise the entire known world.

No matter what is surging now in the inner and outer landscape — no matter how invalid or unworkable your present experience appears to be — you are in the perfect place to begin. You can just start right here and right now. And ignite a revolution.

REDRAWING THE BOUNDARIES

Every woman who heals herself helps heal all the women who came before her and all those who will come after.
Dr. Christiane Northrup

As women, coming into the full expression of our Feminine fire we need to create healthy boundaries.

There are many types of boundaries that are possible. In the outer world we see all sort of boundaries which can act as metaphors for us as we learn to build our own. There are wild hedges, low wooden fences, ornate metal railings, brick walls, bamboo screens or flower borders. There are also ten-foot-high walls topped with barbed wire and sniper guns, fierce guard dogs, and signs saying: "Trespassers Will Be Prosecuted". Each invites a certain sort of way of relating — one says: "I have something to defend and see you as a potential attacker", the other says: "This is my space, please enter respectfully".

In the wise words of Bethany Webster, "Healthy boundaries are **'selectively permeable.'** They are not too rigid nor too loose (not extreme). Rather, they are flexible and can be opened or firm when needed, much like a healthy cell." Boundaries keep us safe when they need to, contain our energy, and allow us to stay open to that which is life-giving.

Some people have no respect for boundaries, and therefore barbed wire may be needed to keep you safe. Others will see the low bushes and realise this is your space. But many of us don't even plant the flowers. We have been taught that to be liked, to be Good Girls, we must be nice to everyone. And so we have the hearts of our homes and ourselves laid out on the main road. Many of us have been taught that we should let anyone who wants walk in our front door in their muddy shoes and help themselves to our cookie jars without asking us. We don't do this in our homes, and our bodies are more precious, more vulnerable and powerful than these. Fully armed and defended we will never be able to co-create with others, to learn and grow, trust and flourish. Without boundaries we will be taken advantage of and our energy will belong to everyone else. Without boundaries the power coming through us will leak out, and we will not be able to consciously focus and direct it. We need to find a way of laying boundaries clearly, raising them if needed in certain times with certain situations, and learn not to set up camp in the middle of a war zone.

UNFREEZING

Our global borders have been progressively opened over the past decades, and the same has happened on a personal level. Through the internet we are exposed to more and more people of different experiences, beliefs and characters on a daily basis. But in the midst of this new freedom there is a counter-surge — one to shut down and control out of fear of attack. As Burning Women many of us have experienced this personally. First we move out into the world with our work, perhaps after years of being too scared, and suddenly an unseen attack leaves us feeling exposed and vulnerable. Our old defence structures kick in. Trauma awakens. We freeze.

This is happening on an individual and collective level, right now. The old structures of defence are proving not to work in this hyper-connected world. The temperatures are rising — in the environment and in our cultures. The cracks are showing.

What once held us frozen and solid in fear, is melting, releasing all the power it has been storing. We are being confronted with all these things we have been defending ourselves from or ignoring over generations. We are being forced to deal with what we have been blocking.

Once an energetic block is located and accessed, the matter transmutes into pure energy that we gain into our systems once more. Furthermore, it is not blocking the flow of our energy, which further frees us up. This is why approaching and finding ways to heal energy blockages in the body and psyche is so important — we may feel great resistance in the lead up, because of the fear of reawakening old trauma, but facing it is usually much quicker and less painful than holding it, and it is massively energising.

We have been taught to dichotomise, within patriarchal thinking, to distinguish good energy (for example, excitement) from bad energy (anxiety). And so we try to attach to the "good", and try to avoid the "bad", rather than realising that it is all simply energy, which must flow through our systems.

A powerful experience in the week after I had had the car crash I mentioned earlier, brought home to me in greater clarity than ever before, just how arbitrary our divisions were. In that week I experienced shock, fear, orgasm, anxiety all simply as energy pouring through my body — each with their own emotional overtone, their own stories, each activating certain parts of my body more than others, but each was just energy, pure energy. My role, I saw in great clarity then, just as I had in birth, was allow the energies to pass through me, not to block or resist, and not to get attached to the emotional hues or the stories, simply to allow the energy to pass through, which the body tends to do by shaking.

All energy, whether anger, fear, anxiety, creative, spiritual or sexual energy comes from the same source — and it is all just passing through. We need to learn how to allow ourselves to feel it fully as it does so, and then we, as Burning Women, learn how to focus it creatively — perhaps through art, or confrontation, or activism, through body work or making love and channel it through us and out into the world.

Burning Woman, as a woman of big feelings and clear perception, is by necessity a woman aware of her suffering and that of others. She is a woman who feels the pain of the Earth herself. Burning Woman is she who knows how to work with this pain — to heal it, to creatively transmute it into beauty, love and deeper connection.

The role of the Burning Woman is deeply challenging because our world is so full of pain and suffering right now. Because we feel so deeply, it becomes overwhelming and feels easier to freeze ourselves to it, to not look, to not feel it. The more we are numbed, and the more overwhelmed we become, the more terrifying the idea of allowing ourselves to feel any of it, let alone all of it.

But the only way it can be transformed is by our truly seeing and feeling it. By holding space for it. So as Burning Women we need to learn to hold space, and be held in order to feel and transmute pain into power, rather than simply be hurt by it, rather than freezing to it or defending against it.

Because the secret we have been missing is that these old defences did not only defend us from attack, but also from intimacy with the creative process. They kept us not just from hate, but also love. Not just from death, but from life herself.

MOTHERLINE

This is my story.

This is the story of my mother and daughter and grandmother and her mother.

This is our story.

This is the story of finding She who creates and destroys.

In ourselves.

This is the story of untelling the old stories.

This is your story.

We are the daughters of the fire,
We are the mothers of the fire,
We are the sisters of the fire,
We are the Burning Women.

The Burning started before we were born, and will continue long after.
We are her handmaidens.

We did not choose the burning
She chose us.
And it has been hard.
And it has been beautiful.
It separates us
And one day, perhaps, it can unite us.
I feel the fire in my belly.
I am hungry for that day.

The burning goes far back, so too does the instinct to run and hide from it. We each have a seam of Feminine fire running through our ancestral lines which we may well not have seen how to tap into. This is the fire of Burning Woman herself, the red thread, the life blood.

For many women the biggest pain, the deepest energy blockages are between her and her mother, her and her daughter, her and her sister. These are the Motherline wounds. The line, which, when cleared, leads us back to the Feminine source. The idea of the Motherline was first propounded by Naomi Lowinsky and is a powerful model for understanding ourselves in the context of our female lineage.

As Burning Women our maternal lines probably go back through many, many women who shut down to their fire, who were burned by others, and those whose fires burned them, their families and marriages alive. We are the descendants of grandmothers and mothers who each handled the fire in their own way, trying to survive. We have more choices today, so when we choose to claim our power, we do it not only for ourselves, but all our ancestors that could not.

Looking up and down my own Motherline, I see that I come from a lineage of women of fire—women whose energy is seen as too big, too much, in need of control. Women who struggled to inhabit the massive internal power they were born with, in the body and life of a woman in patriarchal culture. Our power has been too threatening, too scary for ourselves and others. We each have struggled with how to express it in the world. We have been mad, bad and sad. And we have created our own magic. We have burned each other and ourselves in this dance of fire —trying to stay true to ourselves, and stay true to our roles of good mothers and daughters in the patriarchal play. Each time we felt trapped in our expression, each time our power has been constrained, physically or emotionally, each of us has found our way through, often leaving scorch marks around her.

The Dark Mother, the Crazy Woman in each of us has been slashing through the walls and barriers, hacking at trip wires and shells to be free. She longs for freedom like air and lashes at all those who she believes constrain her. All she knows, like a wild animal, is the smell of the sea, the openness of the moor, the smoke of the fire, she needs life itself in its pure raw form to stay alive.

She will kill anything that gets in her way. And there is so much in her way. She doesn't care for the world we have been brought into, the subservient roles we choose to play. She sends the images and feelings through us deep and thick—too grand to be kept hemmed in by the mundanity of daily life. They long to be seen, to be heard — they writhe and scream —we sense their power and turn in fear, or come to them, plucking and shaving them before we share them with the world.

And so we become two-faced, the good woman/crazy woman, good mother/bad mother, good girl/bad girl, the seen and the hidden —whirling in fiery battles with each other, or deafening silences. We play these roles out with each other in an entrenched unconscious dance. We each have tried many ways of escape — through madness, depression, illness, shouting, affairs. But none can set us free. Only we can do that, by connecting to our own power, rather than disowning it. We each have our weapon for release — the pen, the brush, the needle.

Too much fire, too close together can be dangerous, or can be incredible, depending on our ability to stay conscious with it. In the midst of our own internal struggles we often forget our sisterhood, and have turned our frustration against each other. Much of the time we are dancing in the dark together but apart —our unconscious shadows, victim darkness, pain bodies, old shames and fears awake and engaged. We are used to this habit, this pattern. How can we break this spell? How can we move beyond it? How can we set ourselves free? How can we speak our truths and not burn the heart of the other? These are the big questions that we as women from lineages of fire must face before the fullness of our own power can be released.

We must learn to stay conscious with the energy. To commit time and again to feel it as it pours through us. To create clear boundaries.

This power can be terrifying. But it holds magic, which can be transformed by the power of conscious attention, by the courage to feel the unfeelable. Feeling brings it from blackness to colour, from fear to love. It doesn't come to hurt, but to transform: blasting away the old and the dead and to reveal life more fully and richly. It is big energy, big magic, waiting to be fully released. This has been our curse, and is our greatest blessing — our gift. We mothers and daughters are finding her voice buried deep in the silence of our mothers and grandmothers. The time has come to let go of the old stories and become the new flame carriers of Burning Woman.

BURNING QUESTIONS ᴪ FIRESTARTERS

THE CALLING

Have you ever experienced a calling? When? Where? What form did it take?

Can you express this through images or writing? What were its key qualities? How did you act on it?

How have you kept to this original calling. . . and how might you have moved away from it? Is the calling still strong for you, or has it gone quiet?

If it has gone quiet, can you allow yourself to cut away everything that is muffling it, so that you can re-experience the vividness of the call?

RECLAIMING YOUR POWER

What in your life energises you? And what drains you?

What makes you feel powerful?

When did you first experience a feeling of being powerful as a child?

Can you recall experiences of feeling powerful as a teen, in your twenties, thirties, recently? What did it feel like in your body? How did you feel about people seeing you in your power?

What caused you to step back from this?

Firestarter

Think of a powerful woman who inhabits her Feminine power. Really bring her to mind — first through active imagination, and then by writing, painting, or embodying her through movement and costume.

How does she look?

How does she sound?

What does it feel like to be in her presence?

Where in her body is her main source of energy?

CONNECTING TO SOURCE

What do you believe your Source of power to be and how do you connect to it?

THE POWER PROCESS

Firestarter

Think about your baptism of fire, or a major transitional event in your life. Write down each part of the power process as a heading and under each write the events that you associate with each part of the process. You may choose to create a picture of each one.

If you are a visual learner why not create a map or illustrated diagram of the stages of the power process for reference and keep it to hand as a reminder.

BOUNDARIES

What do boundaries mean to you?

Do you struggle with creating boundaries —are you too open, or do you cut yourself off?

When have your boundaries been transgressed? How did you respond?

Firestarter

Either in your imagination or on paper, consider what your current boundaries look like now.

Go through the major relationships in your life, and interactions with strangers, and consider whether you have different boundaries for different people. Are there some people who have a tendency to leaving you feeling violated or invaded? Are there some who you are shut down to?

Then bring each of these people to mind once more and consciously create the boundaries in your mind's eye that you now desire. You may choose to have a bomb proof wall for some in your life, and a white picket fence for others. Why not draw them in your journal?

THE MOTHERLINE

How connected do you feel to your Motherline?

Envisage your female lineage going back in your mind's eye: your mother, her mother, her mother's mother. How did each of them burn, and how were they burned?

Firestarter

Create a visual representation of your Motherline using photographs or drawings of all the women on it.

9

EMBODIED INITIATIONS TO POWER

If there is to be a serious advance in the status of Western women, we need a widespread rebellion of women who refuse to play along with society's rigid body expectations any longer, and who are determined to raise their daughters with a positive and healthy body image. This is the final frontier of the women's movement.

Melia Keeton-Digby, *The Heroines Club*

When I studied History of Ideas at university, when I read books on paradigm shifts they always assumed that change happened first on the level of the mind. A revolution of ideas. Good old male *logos*. Not through the body. Certainly not through my personal Feminine body.

But this is what I have discovered: when a woman's body comes alive, everything shifts. Reality shifts. And not just on the level of the mind. The shifting of the unconscious is felt first and most strongly in the body.

The way into our Feminine power is through our women's bodies. Bodies that we have been alienated from for generations. We have been taught to fear them and been shamed about them. As Burning Women our task, again and again, is to get out of our minds and into our bodies in order to connect our innate passion, our primal fire, the source of our power.

Many of the portals we pass through on our way to our

power are laced through or locked by our bodies' remembering of the times we opened and things didn't play out as we had hoped. As we move deeper into our bodies, we must move gently. Respectful and honorific of the passages to power we have already passed through: we are on hallowed ground here. The ground of nakedness and beauty, creativity and birth, sex and orgasm, deep vulnerability. We each have our own stories. Of times when these were forced or prohibited, times when we were shocked or shamed, times when we felt we had failed, losses we have to bear. I do not know your story. But you do. For yourself, for all women, please honour it. Honour your places that feel broken, the physical scars your body bears, the memories your body holds in its cells. Honour these portals to power, see if you can find the courage to allow them to be your access points to healing.

Together we are learning to move from raw emotion and frozen muscles into a flow that emerges deep from within. We are learning to dance our prayers, bleed our words onto the page, laugh our images onto canvas — to transmute and transmit the energy of the Feminine through our bodies and out into the world.

GETTING NAKED

Society INVESTS in us hating ourselves, one of the most powerful ways to stick it to the system is to decide that's just not an option, that hate is a waste of time and you've got bigger things to do. Self-love and self-care are not selfish acts, choosing to love yourself indefinitely and unapologetically is a radical choice that strengthens the climate of justice and positivity in our communities as a whole!
Phoebe Wahl, artist

The feminine, however disguised, is always naked.
Marion Woodman

Taking off my clothes I feel vulnerable
Until I stand here
And you see me
As I am
Dressed in nothing but myself,
Whole in my skin.

The nude female is at the centre of the Western world. Erotic, exposed, perfect, whatever that means at that precise moment in his-story: her body is carved into the form of fashion. From galleries to online pornography and every billboard and magazine the perfect female form is naked for our delight, selling everything from shower gel to sex.

Heterosexual women have been taught to see themselves through the critical male gaze. Our power has been to arouse, to seduce, to meet with approval. To do this we learn to dissect our bodies' wholeness into pieces, to fragment into breasts and butts and hair, which should be slender but round, natural but honed. We are expected to devote ourselves to the cultivation of ourselves as the perfect image.

As Good Girls we are taught to keep our clothes on. A naked body is a temptation, we are taught, it is dangerous. And if it is not perfect, it is shameful. It can pollute society, corrupt the young. It is dirty and unhygienic. We each have had so many shames written on our flesh, that when we uncover our bodies, we uncover those shames.

The naked woman is a beautiful paradox, dependent on the eye of the beholder. She is simultaneously an icon of patriarchal subjugation and Feminine freedom. Same body, different context. If the naked woman in patriarchy is a sexual object, naked for the pleasure of others, to be judged or arousing, the naked woman in the Feminine is naked subject only to herself, naked as a form of self-expression, collective power and wild, natural belonging.

Being naked with others in a non-sexual public context is something which our mainstream culture cannot countenance, but it is one of the cornerstones for reclaiming our sense of power in our embodied selves, of unpeeling shame, and being seen in our own skins. It allows us to start to open to pleasure and sensuality in the body, purely for its own purpose. We learn to please ourselves, to see our bodies as connected to and yet unique from all other bodies, and as grounded in nature too.

Being naked together is one of the most vulnerable and deeply thrilling feelings in life. When you drop your clothes, you drop your ability to hide yourself as you are, to cover your reality with shame and artifice. A woman undressed stands in the fullness of who she is: she embodies herself.

I remember the first time I got naked in a room full of women.

I was twenty-two. And had hated my body for as long as I could remember. It was too fat, too white and I was way out of my comfort zone: in a Japanese public bath house. Women of all ages, but all much smaller than me, were walking around nude, scrubbing each other's backs, washing each other's hair, chatting, laughing, sitting quietly side by side in the pools. There was nothing weird or sexual about it. Just normal women. Naked. Together.

And when I reached beneath my fear and my shame there was a deep resounding voice: *This. Feels. Right.*

When you are naked with others your highly trained instinct of comparison is dropped.

Time and again I have heard this — from people taking part in naked bike rides, naked swims and hikes, steaming in saunas, sunbathing on nude beaches, joining in with ceremonies, art installations, book and film projects: to get naked with others is to free yourself from your cultural conditioning and step into your humanity in a visceral way. To get naked with others is to fully inhabit yourself, and to be united with others in a way that daily life never allows. It is deeply intimate. It allows an expansion of self, an exhilarating sense of real aliveness, and a revisioning of our beliefs about pleasure, sexuality and the body. Suddenly our eroticism embraces the feel of cool air on our breasts, warmth on our bellies, the feel of sand beneath our toes, the water in our hair. Our sensuality is no longer bound to the act of penetration. To be naked is to be naturally ourselves.

Getting naked is a powerful metaphor and literal tool that requires us to step out of their stories and into our bodies as truth. It is a powerful antidote to the powerlessness perpetuated by patriarchy.

MAGNIFICENT

Do you know the feeling when your body becomes your enemy, your own persona seems a traitor?

I get this often. My sense of self dissolves into dust and ashes. Especially when I am in groups of people. I know this. I will it not to happen. I go small and quiet as I feel the boundaries of my self grow cloudy and weak.

Who am I in comparison to all these others? I fall in on myself, words dry to dust and stick in my mouth. The smaller I get the worse I feel. My outer shell is my only giveaway that I am here. I will it to disappear too. It is too big, too fat, too ugly, too messy, too obvious.

I. Do. Not. Belong. Here. With all these happy people, these thin, pretty, talkative real people. These friends. I know they are friends. I know they cannot hate me as much as I believe they do.

But I am stuck in quicksand now. I am a shadow that people have expectations of. They see this shell and think it's me. It's not, it's not. . . I am somewhere else. This flesh is not me.

I want to run but this will mark me out as even more freakish. I plant my feet, toes twitching. I want to run. To hide. I want to scatter to the wind, to become invisible. I feel naked and raw and stupid and scared and very, very alone in the midst of conviviality. I am unacceptable. I want to be accepted. Why does this always have to happen? I find a friendly face and pour myself into communion with one. I can do one to one. In it I can begin to find myself again. I can be known.

*

The camera comes out. My whirling pieces know that they will be captured, seen, compared and judged next to all these real people. I know from experience the more you struggle, the more fuss you make, the more you mark yourself out as the freak, the more you hurt inside afterwards. They want photos. Let them have their photos. Shhhh.

So you position your mountainous, monstrous, flesh doll body of freakdom behind a normal person — a child, a husband, a friend — you tilt your chin up to avoid the triple chin of hell look, you hold your eyes wide, plaster a smile on your face that will make you look weird. But less weird than not smiling.

And then you have to do the obligatory looking at photos. Happy people. Smiling in the sun. Good memories. But all you can see is you. The freak. Everyone can see you. Everyone is pretending that they are not disgusted.

The feeling of shame grows. Shame for being so superficial. So self-centred. For going down this spiral again. And again. For not being able to be normal.

I am fat. I am ugly. My shame is that now EVERYONE can see this. "The more you fuss, the more you draw attention to it, to yourself," I tell myself. "The more you draw fake niceties from those who love you."

You don't want nice. You just want invisibility. Strange for someone who talks loud and interrupts all the time, who dominates and demands attention. For someone who makes their living in the public eye.

The camera does not lie. It captures truth for posterity. Which people show their friends, their family. They show this shell of you, as though it were you. It is, it must be. You can see it, I can see it. . . you cannot argue with a photograph. It shows the ugly truth.

But that truth is not me. It does not represent me. And yet, this cipher will be the "me" you look back at and remember. The shell.

But I was not there.

*

He strokes my lower back with love and desire. I shrink into myself. The shame, the disgust. How can he want this freakish mountainous body? My mind is racing, shame, shame, shame spilling out of every pore. I will myself to be normal, to respond to the love. . . But all I want is to be invisible.

I try to pour my energy, my awareness into my body. A trick I have taught myself to ground my panicking mind. I can't. My body is not safe. My body is the problem. My mind whirrs on faster and faster. My mind is not safe. Where do you go when your body and your mind are the problem? There is nowhere left. It all confirms the truth you are trying to hide. You're a freak, not normal. Normal people are not always at odds with reality. With their very existence.

I will invisibility. Still it does not come. The tears fall faster, breathing gets shallower.

I run.

*

He strokes me gently, gently. The tears fall. I stay there. Gently, gently, he strokes, I stay. Gently, gently I feel my awareness moving down from my head to my belly. It is safe, it is safe.

With every part of himself, with care and passion he brings me slowly, slowly back into myself. He knows me so well. Knows which tears mean stop, and which mean needed release is happening. He knows that when the orgasm is hidden deep and is hard to come by, it is because it is hidden behind armoured flood gates. Its release brings with it floods of tears, and relief. As the tears fall, the muddy waters are turned crystal clear. Strength returns to my body. Every piece of myself is called back to me. I am whole, I am me. My breath comes out deep from my belly, my resistance has melted, my body soft and warm. I am me. Completely. There is no need to compare. I am incomparable.

Magnificent.

The word hits me with full force. I realise the reason I feel too big to be pretty, too strange to be normal, that I don't fit. . . is because I am and I don't.

I am too big. There is too much of me to fit into normal. Fitting into normal shrinks me.

I am big, I am brave, I am a hundred thousand whirling pieces which centre around this soul. I am powerful and vulnerable.

I am not beautiful, pretty, slim, compliant, superficially nice or attractive or any of the other things which society wants me to be. I have to discard parts of me to fit into any of those boxes, and then the rest of the pieces whirl, dismembered.

But when I am here. With you. And you know me. And I trust you.

I am me.

Completely.

And I am magnificent.

THE POWER OF THE WITNESS

In another woman's strength, may we see our own. In another woman's fear, our own becomes acceptable.
Molly Remer

What will it take for you to know yourself as magnificent, to take up the space that is your birthright? For your body to truly become home? For it to become your sacred vehicle for authentic self-expression, rooted in your own authority?

Some of us have never lost this, others have learned it all by ourselves. But most of us first need to be seen, to be witnessed by trusted, loving others, so we can replace the critical gaze in which we have lived our whole lives, with the gaze of deep loving acceptance. As children we learn who we are by how others see us, by reflecting us back to ourselves. As women, we tend not to take over the adult role of witnessing ourselves. We still need to be independently verified. We have to be seen into being. We do not trust ourselves, our bodies, our instincts. We are too terrified of not being the Good Girl.

For most of us being seen holds its own fear of judgement, a sense of deep vulnerability. Those who tend to crave to be seen in this world, are those who are hiding themselves the most, beneath layers of makeup and perfectly styled hair, and the latest fashions. They are longing for approval of their carefully crafted personas.

The witnessing that we are talking about here, is a witnessing of nakedness: body and soul.

The witness takes the place of the mirrors that we tend to look into to see ourselves. Instead of flat glass we see ourselves through the loving eyes of another. Someone who celebrates our unique beauty. Who sees through the surface to the woman who lives under the skin: the sensitive, powerful, passionate, visionary, delicate, messy woman you are who burns with passion and quakes with fear, who eats and shits and pukes and communes with the divine.

It is what every human being most longs for: to be seen and accepted as they are. From toddlers to elders we hunger to be witnessed. To be beheld. To be accepted. To be adored. To know ourselves as holy.

The witness was first the role of our mother, who taught us who we were in the world. But because of issues with boundaries and poor attachment, many of us did not see ourselves clearly reflected in our mother's eyes. Instead we saw ourselves distorted and fragmented in the eyes of a woman far from wholeness. And so as adults we seek out other witnesses who can give us the sense, that each of us need in order to individuate fully. In time we learn to witness ourselves in this way, to become mirrors for ourselves. We learn how to hold space for ourselves, to find our own core stability in the world and become our own authority.

The power of the witness becomes apparent to me again and again in my work. When we are seen and heard in deep acceptance, without judgement, we grow into ourselves.

Witnessing each others' sparks as they come into flame,

We blow on them our belief,

Shelter their nascent vulnerability with our bodies,

Holding space for each other

As we come alive in the dark.

In the witnessing is something sacred which, when given space and attention, begins to unfold and bloom.

First we begin by seeing ourselves as we are now. In total acceptance. Our gentle curiosity allows us to become aware, perhaps for the first time, of that which lights us up on the deepest level. All that has previously lain in the shadow, terrified of rejection or judgement — our own or others' — is finally admissible and acceptable. We allow ourselves to turn each precious part of ourselves over in our hands, learning by heart and honouring that which turns us on to life, discarding all the habits and behaviours we have taken on through aping others, or looking for acceptance: the things we should like, the way our voices should sound or how we should look. We feel our own body's urges and idiosyncrasies and heed them, perhaps for the first time. We allow ourselves to lead the dance to our own rhythms. We open our mouths to tell our own stories. Until we are continually creating ourselves in our own image, making our lives our own works of art.

OPENING OUR MOUTHS, SPEAKING OUR TRUTHS

We must find words. . . or burn.
Olga Broumas, Artemis in *Beginning with O*

I have a recurring dream: I am standing on stage, I open my mouth. . . and nothing comes out.

This is the vulnerability of opening our mouths, our hearts: what if when we do, nothing is there? What if when we do we cannot break the silence? What if everyone is watching when we open and we fall apart? What if they laugh? What if we fail?

Midwife Ina May Gaskin notes with interest, from her decades of observing women in labour, that when we close our mouths and our throats, the other end closes down too: we clench our vaginas and wombs. They work in unison. An open throat and an open cervix allow a free flow of energy and power through our bodies. Constriction of either stalls the process of labour — which is, ultimately, oneness with the power of the life force. So when we are silenced from expressing ourselves through shame or fear, either through our yonis or our voices, we become shut off from our source power.

The opening required for Burning Woman is a simultaneous inner and outer opening — a sacred agreement not to shut down and hide anymore, a conscious decision to become more fully embodied on every level. It is simultaneously thrilling and terrifying.

Opening in authentic vulnerability is a cracking of the

patriarchal shell. It is a refusal to wear a mask, project a persona, hide in silence or shame. It is a powerful act of creative rebellion. It can leave us feeling very vulnerable, which is why it is so important to ensure we start the process in safe space.

Just as we need to be seen into being. So too we need to be heard.

Magic happens when we open our mouths and dare to break the silence we have been holding. It is as though she has been waiting for our voices to engage her frequency: all sorts of unseen possibilities begin to unfold and appear. When we dare to speak our truths, to call in what we most desire, when we honour our stories we spit out the secondhand lessons of fear that we have swallowed down as Good Girls, and replace them with our own lived truths.

When we open our mouths and speak our truths out loud — whether for the first or the fiftieth time — our voices may shake, our bodies may quake.

Often we feel that if we are shaking, it is because we must be afraid and weak. Because powerful people are strong, unshakeable, they don't get scared. Or if our message were stronger, or clearer, or perhaps if we just tweaked it to make it more acceptable to the world, then we wouldn't be standing here shaking like a leaf, feeling like we're going to vomit and pee at the same time. And so we step back, or start to desperately change our message or ourselves. We try to control our voices, our bodies, take something to "steady our nerves". Anything to stop the shaking.

But what if you knew that this was normal? This is okay. There is nothing wrong with you. This is simply your whole body being filled with the fullness of the life force about to be birthed through you. This is the blessing of Feminine power rushing through your veins shaking you open, in order to shake the world awake. Do not fear it. Do not shame yourself as being crazy. You are not.

And so Burning Women learn in time to rest into the shaking, rather than run from it. We learn to be gentle with ourselves when we feel it. We learn to stop second guessing ourselves, relax our throats, ground the energy, breathe deep into our bellies, open our hearts and step forward. Until suddenly we realise it's not going as planned. We may hear strange, uncomfortable images emerging from our lips, vulnerable stories asking to be shared, or our words dry up and the tears are falling. This is not what we signed up to. Shame and fear rise up once more. We wanted to be powerful women, holding the podium. Except... wait a minute. We've fallen back into the trap again, of other people's authority eclipsing our own. Almost every speaker we've ever seen, we suddenly realise, has been standing on the male stage, speaking in a male voice, with carefully crafted words and a beautifully polished persona.

But here you are, Burning Woman, raw and vulnerable, called to speak from the heart. You were judging it all by the patriarchal ideas of The Expert: the embodiment of unquestionable authority and masculine power. You know what, it's okay to be YOU, love, exactly as you are. You don't need your silly hat or your grand title. You don't need to be rich. You don't need their permission. If you've been invited, you show up, and you stand there in your power without apology. Just showing up and opening your mouth in authentic vulnerability is revolutionary. There is no authority you need to assert or appease. You are standing here in it. Nothing is as you feared it would be, now you are rooted in the Feminine. The stage. The audience. The message. The purpose. The language... and your voice. All are transformed. You are free.

As Burning Women we learn, time and again, that our commitment is not to pleasing others, but to expressing our own understanding of Source as clearly as we can. To do this we realise that we must find our own words, our own language in order to most effectively share our own truth.

Our words and images are both our end goal and our tools for the journey. Learning our own language and speaking it often with others is our purpose. At each stage we reclaim deeper and deeper layers of our individual expression of the Feminine as we dig down to find the wellspring, the Source. All the way down we express what we find: our eroticism, our creativity, our spirituality, our sense of connection to ourselves, our shames, our fears, each other and the world in our own words and own images.

What emerges may look strange to our eyes, and the eyes of the world at first sight, because it has never been seen before. It has been hidden and silenced and sanitised. We have not been allowed to open to what lies beneath in a long, long time. It may be covered in dust and cobwebs and bits of caul and blood and shit, but it is perfect as a newborn baby. Cradle them gently, love them fiercely, these treasures from the deep. And share them. Share them fully, let them be witnessed, dear midwife of the Feminine.

Do not underestimate the courage that this opening takes or how much overcoming it requires. It is something which most of our mothers, grandmothers and great-grandmothers before us would not have been able to consider. It requires that we cast aside generations' worth of programming and limitation.

Breaking our silence is powerful. Whether it comes as a whisper or a squeak at first, allow that sense of spaciousness, of opening, allow yourself to trust the bottomlessness, and lean into the dark roar which will light up every cell.

Though it may start softly, as we build in confidence and skills, we realise we do not need to wait for permission before we open our mouths. We do not need to wait for others to make space for us, we can take it. We do not need to read from others' scripts or style ourselves in weak comparison. We do not need to look to another's authority because we have our own. Down in our cores. We have waited so long for permission to know that it was our time, our turn on stage. That time is now. Our voices are being heard into being. They are needed.

OPENING DEEPER—EROTIC INITIATION

The erotic is an assertion of the feminine life force, of creative energy empowered.
Audre Lorde

The personal reclamation of the female body and the sexuality within it, is the fourth wave of the feminist movement.
Sheila Kelley

The dark flame
Rises from below.
The orchid of fire
Is blooming now.
Earth her body,
Flames her passion,
Opening, spreading,
Intoxicated with splendour
She erupts into a
Shower of galaxies.

There is no faking nor controlling the erotic Feminine. No wonder she has been caged and forbidden by patriarchy. The erotic body is fully open and alive with pure energy. In ecstasy we experience the beauty of total surrender to life herself. The erotic is a key way into connecting to Source power and releasing it into the world. Through our erotic bodies we learn to channel, build up and discharge energy, and release the physical blocks which hold it in place and embark on a process of active surrender, a journey into openness, towards sensation, away from the mind.

Discovering our own erotic selves and learning to work with this energy, and translate it into other areas of our work is a key part of Burning Woman's role. Through the erotic we learn to access bigger, stronger surges of energy into our bodies. When energy starts to move in the body it tends to call to be released erotically. The physical release of the muscles in our lower torso where the base chakras are situated, allow for the increased charge to flow throughout our whole systems.

The erotic is often synonymous with sex — but we can experience sex without the erotic, and the erotic without sex. The erotic includes experiences in nature; pleasurable elemental experiences on the skin—especially with fire or water; birthing and breastfeeding; dance... The erotic is primal, a direct encounter between Source energy and body. Pre-*logos*, pre-linguistic. *Eros* is the fire of life herself co-creating blissfully through with us.

During erotic opening we learn to be surrendered, to intermingle our energy with that of another, to follow the divine superhighway of pleasure. In erotically charged lovemaking, the masculine and feminine energies (whatever the gender identities of the partners involved) move out from their physical shells and merge. Then we experience the alchemical bliss of union, not only in ourselves but with another. We become pleasure and power embodied.

Burning Woman is one whose body is alive to her sexually, who inhabits and expresses her own eroticism. She learns that a powerful voice and body are rooted in powerful sexual expression. She advocates for her own pleasure and hungers in bed, and the world beyond.

In the masculine system, pain, violence and the erotic have been disturbingly mingled. Pleasure is only acceptable as long as we suffer in some way for it. See the alarming sales of *50 Shades of Grey* — when mainstream women leapt hungrily at a culturally acceptable access point to the erotic. Naturally it was through the degraded and abused body of a woman in an interpretation of sado-masochistic practice, so that they learned the lesson once more that to be a woman is to suffer.

We have a strange relationship with pain, no doubt in part a relic of the belief in pain as punishment for the sin of having been born human, from the Christian idea of martyrdom, depicted in the disturbing agony of Christ on the cross. This has translated into the doctrines of capitalism and patriarchy that require pain and sacrifice: the cuts of austerity for the greater good. We become martyrs to pain in order to prove our strength. We learn that we cannot be powerful without extreme suffering and hardship. And so we push ourselves too hard, discipline ourselves and whip ourselves into shape so that we can become more powerful. Don't believe me? Just take a listen in to your inner monologue the next time you are "working hard" or "pushing yourself through". We learn to numb ourselves to the pain — through painkillers and addictions and overwork, to prove ourselves powerful and strong, not weak women. We fear the raw sensations of the feeling body, and aim for controlled numbness.

And the more numb we become, the more pain we have to feel before we react, the more recognition we get. We learn to wear our pain as a badge of honour. We learn to push on. To work harder. But our female bodies soon teach us that this cannot, will not, work for them. Whether we tear during childbirth, have recurrent bouts of mastitis, or burnout takes us down, our bodies tend to have to reach screaming point before we heed their pleas to stop.

The way of the Feminine is revolutionary because it asks that rather than pain, we fuel ourselves with pleasure. Rather than force, we cultivate a playful approach, we learn to open gently at first, then ecstatically. Rather than numbness we choose to feel. Our opening is not forced, but is hormonally fuelled by oxytocin—the hormone of love and connection. This opening is juicy and led by our own appetites, our own desires.

We have denied our own pleasure for so long, leaving it at the bottom of to-do lists, waiting to be earned, as a reward. We have believed the lie that tells us we have to do something, be something more, in order to deserve pleasure. We do not believe that we deserve it as our birthright. It is always somewhere off in the distant future. Not here and now.

To awaken to the Feminine a woman has to lay down her addictions to numbness. She has to learn to feel and not stay stuck in the stories of these feelings, but to feel each emotion fully as it flows through her. She must learn to trust her feelings as her inner compass: her anger, her pain, her sadness, just as much as her joy, her desire and her gratitude. She does not get to choose the so-called "positive" emotions, without the "negative": to allow deep pleasure requires vulnerability. Vulnerability allows for the risk of real pain, genuine suffering. Not the pain she has been taught to seek in a masochistic way of the masculine, to toughen her up, and prove her strength. But to love deeply, to feel deeply, opens her to the risk of losing that which she loves.

Burning Woman learns to consciously seek out and cultivate more and more pleasurable experiences which have previously been denied her. She must do this until she learns to cherish the warm glow on her inner-skin rather than fear it. She responds to the pleasures of her body, privately at first, then building in trust she shares these pleasures little by little with a wider circle. She must learn what gives her pleasure and then fill herself full. And then she learns to share pleasure with those she loves from her fullness, inclusive of herself and her desires—not sacrificing herself for the pleasure of others.

As Burning Women we have to gently watch ourselves as we slip into old habits of seriousness, self-harm, forcing, and remind ourselves that the only way that truly serves us is that of pleasure and playfulness. There may be moments in each day when seriousness serves, but when it becomes habitual, when we live a life of forced, non-pleasurable action, dictated by the will of others, we have lost our way, we have dropped our connection to ourselves and Source. Each time we need to stop ourselves, and gently allow ourselves to release the need to control. To release the fear that is driving us, allow the armour to fall, and allow ourselves to feel once more. To slip back into the groove of pleasure, the drip of honey, the flow of love, the fire and the darkness.

BIRTHING INITIATION

Through our encounters with the erotic, we can find ourselves harbouring new life, giving our bodies and our energy to the creation of something new and never-before seen. Whether a baby or other creative project, our female bodies have the potential to become full and ripe with burgeoning new life.

The process of birth is an embodied experience still common to the majority of women and one that provides a useful metaphor for the transformational energetic process which Burning Women go through. Whether or not you yourself are a birth mother in this life time, through the stories of other women, books and film, birth is a process which you will be, to some extent, aware. Birth is also a uniquely female experience. But our stories of birth have become so medicalised, so detached from our other rites of transformation, that it is easy to forget that birth is a natural process of creativity, with its own rhythms and patterns, and its own wisdom to teach us.

The process of birth starts years before the day we labour. We learn about faith and despair when we struggle with infertility, and patience and hope as we wait for the process of development to go on unseen in the darkness. And when we approach the time where our bodies must release what we have created out into the world we learn courage and surrender. These are the teachings of birth.

Birth is one of the deepest and most powerful openings of any woman's life: physically and energetically. For a lucky few in this world — myself included — it is a true initiation in opening to our Feminine power. But I also want to acknowledge that for all too many it is deeply traumatic: at a time of her deepest opening, a woman is wounded, shamed, numbed, cut open or deemed powerless. For many, whether by choice or circumstance, birth is very different to the one I describe below. I write this mindful of the levels of caesarean sections —planned or unplanned —that circumvent the process I will be describing. If this is your truth, please know that I honour your experience. And please read on with extra gentleness in your heart for all of our various journeys. Like with our mother wounds, birth is a major initiator of Feminine power, just not always in the way we had envisioned for ourselves. If your own birthing journey was traumatic, know that it is never too late to touch the power of transformation that birth brings us. The healing may happen years after the birth itself, as you find support and witnesses to help you heal and release the energies that you could not process at the time.

In every birth — biological or creative — we wander in the terrain between the worlds, feeling our way along the Motherline, to bring another life through. During many births the thinness of this veil between life and death, spirit and matter, becomes clear if we allow it. And if we are not acted upon or traumatised. We walk to the brink, to the edge of our courage, to the edge of the known world, and the women we thought we were. We shed our clothes, our inhibitions and our bodies open. And there in the centre of the blood and the pain, we find the women we are: deeper, stronger, more powerful, more vulnerable than we may ever have imagined.

So let us take a little time together now to explore the energetic process of birth in closer detail.

The first recognizable sign of labour is usually contractions, those first surges of womb power from our Feminine heart of darkness, which bring us to full attention. We realise the extent of power which is shaking us awake. And this is only the warm up. We quickly learn that the more we resist and control, the more pain we experience. We each find our ways to surrender to the energy pouring through us, through movement or sound or breath or visualization or all of them together. We ride these waves of energy for minutes or perhaps days, as the cervix opens wider and wider, until it feels like the world will fall out of us and our bodies will explode.

Any wise midwife can tell you that you have reached transition when you are cursing and crying and saying you can't continue. This is the threshold. This is No Man's Land. Where no man has ever walked. This is where we get to in each creative project, each meaningful relationship, just before each orgasmic climax, that moment of overwhelm, of too much, of *Stop or I will die.*

You have a choice here — you walk through the portal. Or you turn around and walk away.

Except in birth it's not a real choice: the baby must be born somehow.

When you choose to push, if you choose to push, it may be blessed relief or you may wonder how you can possibly do it. But the internal pressure is too great not to. This is when you realise that it is not just you in this process. You sense the baby's head descending, you are working in partnership with the forces of nature — contractions, gravity and new life urgently pressing to be born.

The baby's head crowning stretches the vaginal tissues more than they've ever been stretched before (unless you're into very unusual sexual practices!) They feel like they are burning. This is known as the ring of fire. You may feel as if your flesh is being torn apart. And there's this two-fold urge. To push on, to get through it, to see your baby and finally be done with it — and the urge to stop, and back away. And really you have to do both. At the same time. To keep pushing — gently, compassionately, with your breath and the waves of contractions — for your body, with your body — to match your effort to the waves, and then ease off when the urge to push recedes, to sink into the darkness and rest.

Standing in the ring of fire, the eye of the storm, the vortex of pain and pressure is simultaneously the most vulnerable and most powerful place to be. Here we embody paradox. We stand our ground and surrender completely. Here we know the full power of Feminine fire.

And then our baby is born, and the intensity is over. We have our gift: this new life we have been focused towards for so long. And yet we realise, in this bittersweet moment, that the gift was the process, the act of co-creating with the unknown, of opening and surrendering, which has silently and unseen gifted us something else — a fuller sense of self. We are delivered more deeply to ourselves and woven more profoundly into the web of life.

BIRTHING ON A PLANETARY LEVEL

To spin the web and not be caught in it... to create the world, to create your own life, to rule your fate, to name the grandmothers as well as the fathers, to draw nets and not just straight lines, [...] to be able to sing and not be silenced, to take down the veil and appear.
Rebecca Solnit

Let ecstasy dance you to oblivion.

Hands to your belly, you feel the warmth of your womb

As it pulsates

Giving birth to a burning new world.

Whether we are called to be mothers in this life time or not, all of us as Burning Women are being called to help birth a new world by birthing ourselves. We sense it in our bones, feel the contractions in our bellies. It is our time. Our birth into our own power is moving apace with the planetary birthing. At times the sheer intensity of the process, inside and out, can feel deeply overwhelming.

There are massive energies pulsing through us all right now. Many astrologers of all backgrounds are charting these shifts in the planets. We, especially the highly sensitive amongst us, are experiencing wave after wave of grief. We are being called to let go and heal childhood traumas, disputes, family issues. On a cultural level economies are staggering, wars flaring, climate change bringing a constant deluge of extreme weather. Old power structures are falling. And dangerous demagogues rising. Whether by divine design, because of a shift in the ages, or simply as part of our evolution as a species, we are experiencing change on a much faster level than ever before. Something big and unnameable is moving through us all. A new consciousness which is still nameless and formless.

Those in the System, would like us to share their belief that all these changes are not connected: they are simply anomalies, isolated symptoms to be treated or preferably ignored, before the all-powerful Western capitalist patriarchal model goes on to ever greater heights and grander ejaculations. Most are numb to it, caught in fear, denial or resistance.

But we, Burning Woman, know this process intimately. Amongst Burning Women and Men, there is a fierce, quiet knowing that these are both the death pangs of the old, and the birthing pangs of the new.

We are being asked again and again, in every area of our lives, from business to relationships: do I want to be loyal to my own personal pain and history, or do I want to contribute to collective growth and healing? Do I want to defend the old and outworn modes of power, government and engagement, which are being shown as impotent and dysfunctional, or am I willing to open to the unknown?

It is more than just your or my personal journey, dearest Burning Woman, though that is integral to this process. It is a shift in the global structure of power and the energy we run on. That change is not separate from us. It is one and the same thing.

The time is now. The air is thick with change. A collective roar is rising internally, ready to break through the old shell.

Just like birthing mothers and dying men, we need to stay out of fear, out of defence, resistance and retaliation. Breathe deep into our bellies, let go of our man-made minds and surrender to life.

Raw/Roar

Can you hear it?

The collective roar is rising from our bellies.

Raw Feminine energy

Rising up

Rising freely.

Our throats are open,

No longer strangled shut

Into the helpless silent scream of the prey.

Feet grounded,

We pray,

Fire from our bellies emerging clear through our mouths:

The roar of anger

The roar of birth

The roar of the wild

She-lion, tiger-woman, dragon-sister

Circle

The hurricane rises.

BURNING QUESTIONS & FIRESTARTERS

GETTING NAKED

How did you feel in your naked body—as a child? As a teen? In your twenties? Thirties? Now?

Have you ever felt shamed in your naked body? How did you respond?

When have you felt powerful in your naked body?

Have you ever felt truly seen in your naked body in a non-sexual way? In a sexual way? How did this feel to you?

What does nakedness bring up for you? What does it mean to be seen? Who are you naked? What is embodied vulnerability?

Firestarter

Take your clothes off and look at yourself in the mirror. Listen out for your critical voices and just observe them, then thank them for their concerns, and imagine turning down the volume.

Take some charcoal or pastels and sketch-paper and begin to sketch what you see. You may choose to do it completely accurately, or begin to embellish your favourite features, add symbols which are meaningful to you. Be playful and loving as you pour this naked vision of yourself onto paper. Then take some time to look at what you have created, reflect on what the process of looking and drawing has brought up in you, and write this down.

OPENING YOUR MOUTH

What are your most memorable experiences of opening your mouth?

When have you been shamed for it? Have you fully healed from this?

SHAKING

Have you experienced shaking and been able to identify it as part of the transformational or birthing process, rather than as something to be afraid of?

What do you tell yourself about yourself when your body or voice shakes? What negative messages have you internalised about it? Who or where did they come from?

Shaking is a key for healing trauma — whether allowing yourself to shake as you remember a traumatic event, or as you cry. There is even an entire meditation technique devoted to shaking.

THE EROTIC

What is the erotic to you? Can you express it visually or in words? Can you remember your first connection to it? What was your connection like in your childhood? Teens? Twenties? Thirties? Now?

What does pleasure mean to you?

How often do you allow yourself to fully experience pleasure? When and why do you stop yourself from experiencing it?

What do you believe will happen if you express yourself fully and receive lots of pleasure?

What do you love to play? What reasons do you make not to play? What comes before play?

BIRTHING

What came up for you as you read this chapter? If you have been pregnant and given birth, what was your experience? Which aspects made you feel empowered? And which made you feel disempowered?

How have you experienced the birthing process in other areas of your life beyond childbirth?

Firestarter

How can you express what it means to give birth?

Bring to mind the feeling of birth and allow it to pour out through you in whatever form it calls for — be it writing, painting, sculpture, dance.

10

BURNING WOMAN CEREMONY

Coming home to myself,
Loving eyes to see me.
Giving birth to myself,
Open arms to greet me.
I belong to myself,
I am free, free, free.

ALisa Starkweather, chant

Welcome Burning Woman. Welcome home to yourself. What a journey it has been, and yet the journey is only just beginning.

Now is the time to slip out of your mind and into your own skin. Out of this book and into your life.

It is time, sister, to dance around the bonfire, naked. It is time to live the metaphor as reality.

Many cultures around the world have traditions involving fire, from ceremonial fire circles to walking on burning coals. Each of them is a sacred spectacle and a ritual container for celebration and transformation. In each the fire is a great teacher about overcoming our fears and a visceral way to touch our power.

In the Burning Woman ceremony, we take some of our most entrenched fears: the dark, our voices, being seen naked, speaking our truth, dance, ritual, being judged, not being in control, women's circles. . . We commit to show up. In a held sacred space.

We let ourselves be seen and heard and held and naked. To be witnessed as we are.

And the simple act of showing up, witnessing and being witnessed, teaches us many lessons. Namely that we have nothing to fear. That our fears are merely paper tigers which go up in flames with the first match.

We are more powerful than them. We have given them our power. But we are enough. We are more than enough. We are magnificent. Beautiful in our vulnerability. Powerful in our courage.

Standing in circle with others allows us to see that we all shrink from the same fears. We all burn with the same fire. We are made of the same blood and bones. We have the same dreams. And the only thing holding us back is the stories we tell ourselves of the monsters that hide in the dark. The stories we tell ourselves about ourselves and others. And we know that now is the time to let them go. With love and gratitude, playfulness and reverence, and fire.

Like yesterday's newspaper our stories do not tell the story of who we are today, or what we are becoming. We watch them take light, and we feel the warmth on our bellies as all the stored energy is released. We understand this as a metaphor for the internal processes we have been experiencing. We reabsorb this energy through our skin, our eyes, grateful for its warmth and light. We realise that it is safe, it is necessary, to let our old skins fall away like the autumn leaves. It is beautiful to release. We are safe, we are held, we are loved as we give birth so freely and gently to ourselves. We have to let it all fall away to feed the fire within that will fuel who we are becoming. We stand naked in the fire and allow it to light a spark within us that will burn deeper and truer than ever before.

Shimmering beauty
Untouchable and whole,
Light the way.
Fragments of myself,
Are found and burned.
The fire wholes them.
Our stories burn,
The newspapers of yesterday
Written with the pens of others
On our bodies.
The fire separates the words from the paper,
Sending them up as smoke.
What will you write on your own clean bones?
Who will you be, Burning Woman,
Now the pen is in your hand?

CREATING RITUAL

The Burning Woman ceremony is the opportunity to physically step into everything that we have been discussing.

As I said at the beginning of this book, this ceremony had been calling my name for almost seven years, waiting for me to have the courage to do it. Finally one mid-October evening, as I was struggling alone in the dark writing this book, I was stuck and knew my understanding of Burning Woman needed to be somatic, not just mental. I could not write the middle part of the book unless I had embodied the Burning Woman archetype through this ceremony. And I could not do it alone. I needed a circle of sisters holding powerful ceremonial space with me.

For years I had thought about the ceremony, sure that

thinking it would be enough. But we do not give birth through our minds but through our bodies. I knew this, but still I was scared. Thinking and writing come easier to me than doing.

But it was time, time to step into my power and do what scared me most.

I had over a decade's experience of creating ceremonies at this stage, and they come to me very naturally and intuitively, once I have set a date. And so I checked the weather and my calendar, called in my circle of sisters and trusted that whoever needed to be there would be.

The fire gives us back to ourselves.

In the dark we crawl back into our skins.

The night, a shawl of milk drop stars, clothes us.

Shadows dance, sparks fly.

This body. These stars. These words.

These trees. These breasts. This life.

All yours.

Let your life burst into flames.

The weaving of a ceremony holds power in itself. There is a natural building of energy and anticipation through all the preparations and these should be done in the spirit of the ceremony, not with stress or hurriedness. Preparing the space is a way of preparing ourselves: each action we take is meaningful and ceremonial, adding energetic charge to the space and to our understanding of the ceremony. The process is the purpose.

When you are planning, go and seek out your space. Stand in it, see if it feels right to you. If it is your land, cut back the dead wood, clear the paths, lay the fire circle, work the earth — the clearing happens both on a practical and an energetic level. Get a sense of the space and how it will hold you, what your needs are that must be met—for warmth, safety, a dry space to sit. . .

As you prepare the space you may want to practise singing the songs or chants that you will use so that you are charging the space with your voice. Share the set up with your sisters if you can. You may want to smudge the space with sage or incense, shake rattles or whatever works for you in clearing the space and charging up fresh energy.

So often people start by planning what they will do in a ceremony—the activities that will make up the main body of the event. And whilst I will offer you many possible suggestions, both in the list below, and in the outline of our own ceremony, your ceremony will be far more powerful if you stand in your own power to co-create it, rather than copying the template of another. I remind you to start from your intention for yourself (and the women there) and from the space itself. *What* you do is not as important as *how* you do it. It is the energy that is created and how it is held that makes the ritual meaningful and memorable, and which will start an inner process of transformation that will continue to unfurl for days and months beyond the ceremony itself.

So first set your date—this and the space you have prepared are the containers, waiting for you, holding space. Many women choose auspicious dates to celebrate a fire circle: an equinox, solstice or cross-quarter festival, the opening or closing of a gathering, a new or full moon.

It is crucial to make safe space to hold ceremony in. This, more than anything else, is the aim of this ceremony. You need a space in which it is safe to be vulnerable. Even if you never light a fire or take off your clothes, to have created safe space is a revolutionary act, and deep gift for yourself and every woman who enters it.

Establishing safe space relies on creating strong, supportive boundaries from the very beginning. So only invite those you trust to join you in sacred space. Let them know the time and date, a very simple explanation of your intention, and that it will include nudity. Request their confidentiality so that every woman who joins you is free from shaming and feels safe to come and be present there. Once people have responded, then send out a more detailed invitation with the location and practicalities—what they need to bring and do to prepare.

Be sure that you hold the ceremony in a place where you feel safe that you will not be overlooked or interrupted. If you are doing it alone have a phone with you and make sure someone knows where you are and when to expect you back.

You may want to be inspired (on a much smaller scale!) by the Burning Man festival. You may spend a day or weekend creating a Burning Woman effigy, or perhaps The Good Girl or Ashen Woman. You might sculpt her out of chicken wire and then cover her with papier maché and have a procession with her first. Or you could stuff old clothes with newspaper, or weave her from willow or make her from mud and straw. If you have space outside, you can burn her too!

You may want to sing or dance or chant or drum around the fire. If you know what you are doing, fire walking or fire eating are powerful spectacles.

Think about your bodies and how you might want to adorn them—with silk scarves or henna tattoos, cold ash mixed with water or body paint.

To ensure the energetic safety of all participants, I suggest the use of basic women's circle guidelines:

> What is said and done in circle, stays in circle.

> Each woman takes responsibility for her own feelings and needs and ask for what she needs.

> We speak from our "I".

And boundaries apply to the fire itself too, which we treat with respect. Be sure that it is safe and appropriate to make fire in your chosen place, use a fire pit or stones to contain the fire, don't leave it unattended, be careful of loose hair, skirts and scarves, and be sure it is safely out before you leave.

You may not have access to a suitable outdoor space, if not, then plan it inside, with an open fire in the fireplace, or lots of candles in the centre of your circle. You can also create an altar or mandala of objects related to fire and burning, and burn offerings or fears over a bowl of sand or water.

I recommend that you stay connected to your own darkness before, during and after the ceremony. Stay aware of your body. Journal in anticipation and after to capture both the content of what happened, but also the energy and power of the event. Watch your dreams around this time.

But most importantly, once you have set safe space, try not to over-plan or over-think it — allow space for it to be what it is. Just show up. All of you, to all of it. Nothing is required of you, but that you show up and trust the process. Burning Woman will be there with flaming bells on — she always gets her invitation!

INVOCATION OF BURNING WOMAN

Burning Woman,
Here I am, ready.
See the old shells of myself, my bones and stories,
The weeds and thorns that have kept me trapped.
Take them all.
Consume and transform them.
Let me warm myself on their fire.
Burning Woman,
Come inhabit me,

Set me alight in my own flame.

Give me courage in the darkness.

I am held.

I am witnessed.

I am powerful.

I am courageous.

I am magnificent.

I burn for myself,

I burn for all women, for all children,

I burn with Burning Men

I burn for the Earth,

I burn with you.

OUR CEREMONY

Come with me now, and I will share with you our very first Burning Woman ceremony. Down through the garden, through the tall trees and into the newer grove beyond.

We went to look for a space to hold our ceremony, thinking we knew where it should be in the field, hidden in the long grass. But as we explored, a more perfect place revealed itself. We cut down the dead wood, the tall weeds, the branches that obscured the way. Now we have a magical women's ceremonial space to use whenever we want, made with love and sisters' hands, in the midst of a grove of trees, for our bonfire circle. Completely sheltered, deeply private. You can hear the sea and the birds and nothing else.

We used branches from the woodland; pebbles from the beach across the bog to make the fire circle; leaves to make an altar; tree stumps for seats; my sister's bowls, made of local clay, to hold the altar candle and as a drinking vessel.

As we set up, we made a seasonal altar of red and yellow leaves, wind-fallen ruby apples, walnuts and a fig we found on our way down to the grove, each chosen for their own beauty, and their symbolism — here too is an important place for metaphor. The fallen leaves for what we were releasing, the apples both nature's bounty but also Snow White's apple, and Eve's apple. The fig to represent Eve in the Garden of Eden, and also the female genitalia — in Italian *fica* — fig, is another word for vulva.

We arranged them as a mandala with a candle at the centre. We put tea lights in jam jars along the path and had some with wire wound round the top of the jars to make lanterns. Scarves were hung on the trees and a drum and guitar waited for us.

We laid the fire together, waiting until we were all gathered to light it. Then we sat on logs and sang together, weaving improvised tunes as the rooks flew home to roost, the smaller birds hopped from branch to branch around us cocking their heads in curiosity. The October sky turned from blue to fire red, and dusk started to settle. In the background the ocean waves roared. A bat circled our space in the twilight, the birds quietened as the cooler damp air descended.

I met our other participant and led her down, through the path amongst the trees, weaving down the candlelit way, until we emerged through the opening — the journey was meant to be a sort of rebirth, pushing our way through the last branches and out into the candlelight.

And then the ceremony unfolded. We grounded ourselves in the space with deep belly breaths, held hands to connect together, and sang a circle chant as we lit the fire. . .

There's a circle surrounding, the circle we are in. . .

Round and round it went, the circle of women encircled by the grove of trees, encircled by the sea, encircled by the darkness and the stars. We were connected to ourselves, to each other and to all of nature around us. As the flames started to grow, we stepped back a couple of paces, and each woman shared what she wanted to release, throwing the pages with her words into the fire. And as the heat grew, it was natural to take off our heavy sweaters, and then our tops, to bare our breasts to the warmth, and then our shoes, to feel the cold grass beneath our toes, and then, and then we were nearly there and so our skirts and pants and underwear came off too. I sounded the drums and we began to move around the fire, loving the warmth on our bodies.

I had wondered for so long, *how do you move from normal space, standing there clothed with women you know, to being naked? How does it work?* But the truth is, it just does. And it felt entirely a natural thing to be doing, in the woods, by the firelight and candlelight. We all knew why we were there, we all knew that by showing up, this is what would happen. And so it did.

We enjoyed the fire's glow on our skins, and then we each wrapped the other in silken shawls, an act of embracing our sensuality and caring for each other. The soft fabric on our skins gave us warmth, a sense of being held, to off-set our complete nakedness, so that we could each have our own level of comfort. We each shared a song that we had brought, we said how it felt to be there. We embraced. And then we dressed again, sharing what in our lives we wanted to bring more power to, what of ourselves we wanted to strengthen and celebrate. We passed a cup of hot spiced apple juice with brandy to warm us from the inside and sat in circle together around the dying fire to share our stories.

11

STORIES OF BURNING

Here we are, gathered around the flames together, sitting in circle, a circle of sisters. We have bared our bodies, and from this physical vulnerability comes the courage to stand fully in our souls, to open our hearts and our throats and raise our voices. It is time for our own personal tales of burning to be heard. The stories that have stayed hidden: waiting for sacred space to be witnessed. In these stories lie the seeds of healing, the teachings of souls who have walked through the fire many times, bringing back with them sparks of deep wisdom.

Lean in, closer still, dearest one, until the space between you and these stories narrows, until you know them as your own. This is her-story. This is our story. Stories of Burning Women.

"For years I longed to know what I was here to do, who I was meant to be. I heard other women talking about Burning Woman but I didn't know her myself. But then, once I began to burn I didn't want to let go," one woman with dark hair begins, "it was intoxicating: the sheer joy of finally living on purpose. I became so full of Burning Woman that I lost sight of myself, my husband, my children, my friends. I worked harder, later, said yes to more and more commitments. I burned the candle at both ends: that candle was me. I was on fire and it felt wonderful. I held tight to the fire of Burning Woman, so scared to lose her again.

"As my schedule got fuller, I could feel her pulling away. I could no longer hear her voice as clearly, which made me grasp at her even harder. I felt so stretched I could scream.

But I thought that if I let go the magic would be over, I'd be dead inside once more. I couldn't bear the thought of that. So gradually the playful, wild voice of Burning Woman morphed into the voice of an army sergeant. While I started out doing her work, I was being burned alive by the story I've absorbed over the years about working harder and faster. I was trying to do her work in the only way I knew how, and it was killing my body. It sounds like an exaggeration, but that's what it felt like: my skin was itching, my heart pounding, anxiety ruled my days and my nights. My whole body was inflamed, my body seemed to be allergic to everything. I was tired all the time. But I didn't have the time to be sick.

"The more stretched I was, the more crowded out I felt in my own life. I had forgotten what fun was. Play seemed like a waste of time. I had work to do: her work. But the more I did, the more was left undone. And it felt like I was always last. I was not living what I was teaching. I was ignoring my body's cries for rest, ignoring weekends and holidays, my work mattered, to me, to the world, it became my purpose. And then a cold turned into a deep-rooted chest infection, still I would not rest, trying to do the work of Burning Woman in the way I had always been taught. I forgot that my body was my sacred vessel, it had become a machine ruled by my mind. And I was so angry and resentful when it broke down. I got even more frustrated when my relationships began to shake under the strain. I took everything I could—living off sugar and caffeine, painkillers and antibiotics so that I could keep going. Until one day I couldn't get up. I was exhausted to my bones. Every part of me ached. One day, then another, a week, then another, a month, then two. . . my body was broken, and Burning Woman was still calling my name, but I couldn't get to her. I was caught in a thick fog. All I could do was survive. Her voice was getting quieter and quieter and I could not follow her. I longed for her fire, for the busyness and whirl. I felt tired and old and alone.

I was burned out. And then one day I woke up and found she had gone. I felt dead inside. And I..." her voice trails out as sobs engulf her body.

"Mmmmmm," says an older voice, the poetess, her silver hair reflecting the firelight. Leaning in close to the fire that has begun to sink down into grey ash, she wraps a blanket around her shoulders and strokes the woman's hand.

"This is the time of Ashen Woman. She of the pale face, eyes sunk in their sockets, hair hanging in greasy smoke spirals. Dry as dust she lies, a charred pile of bones on the floor. She is the ghost of the dream, the spirit between fires, the fog in the darkness. Her place is sacred in the burning cycle. She is the one we must visit if we refuse the embrace of the Dark Mother.

"Ashen Woman is she who remains when the burning is done. She whose name we have forgotten or cursed, she whose being has been swept tidily away into the shadows. She is Burning Woman's sister, her twin.

"When the fire has burned through you and left you cold, Ashen Woman is there with you. You who delighted in dancing in the flames. You who were one with the fire that appeared one ordinary Tuesday afternoon and set you ablaze with art and words, the eloquence of poets, the charm of Bathsheba, the erotic energy that pulsed though your veins in ecstatic pulses —you who were one with life, who gave birth to universes, you who were the Goddess' handmaiden, who mistook yourself for Burning Woman herself. You must learn her wisdom, meet her other side. To you she sends her sister, Ashen Woman. But you reject her.

"Your mind is full of burning, you refuse the darkness. You forget to be cradled in it. You call in vain for Burning Woman. Blind and deaf to the wisdom of the Dark Mother."

"Ashen Woman," the first woman responds in a whisper as quiet as the leaves. "That is who I am right now, Ashen Woman. But thinking I should be Burning Woman. I long for

Burning Woman to return, I yearn for her warmth. I long to dance in the flames, again and again, to feel the joy, the fullness of life, the magic of co-creation. . . Oh Burning Woman where are you? Why won't you stay? What have I done to undo the magic, what curses have I brought upon myself? With you I am capable of greatness. Without you I am nothing.

"Oh God, I feel her loss doubly so: I hate my own smallness and shadow, when I know just how vibrant I can be. I am alone surrounded by the dry dust of what has been. Where once there were dreams and visions, now there is only death and silence. My world is crumbling around me. I am here, but I am not here. All I want is to be still, but I can't, there is so much to do.

"I scrabble in the ashes, pushing them aside, choking in the dust which covers everything, but not even an ember remains. How can I summon Burning Woman up once more? Where does she come from and how? Where does she go to and why?"

The older woman puts her arm around her shoulders.

"This is her lesson, my love, that we are neither Burning Woman, nor Ashen Woman, we are never just one thing or another, but a rainbow of woven threads, a kaleidoscope of archetypes. When we first see an archetype or know ourselves in a label, it is like finding a magic mirror: we see ourselves for what feels like fully for the first time. But it is just a mirror. The archetypes can hold a mirror, nothing more. They cannot define us in our totality. We are multi-dimensional beings. When you lose her, it is just her reflection in yourself you have lost. She goes so that you do not forget yourself in your identification with her. She longs for you to be yourself, in your unique fullness of being. She loves to play with you, to come through you. But there are many other parts of yourself you need to share too. It is time for you to return to the darkness, to find the other facets of yourself that the world longs for.

"So sit in the darkness right now, my love, be in that place of emptiness within emptiness. See the ashes, and rather than looking for Burning Woman, look for the burning within yourself. Look for the glimmer of light, the joy and magic which are yours alone," she gestures with her hand towards the fire circle, which had gotten cooler and greyer since they started to speak. "Let your tears out, let them rain down on the ashes.

"Now put your finger there into the ashes and draw it through them. Just move your finger through them and watch. Don't judge. Watch with gentle curiosity as the tears and the ashes combine, the grooves become riverbanks, the ashes become your tea leaves, a picture emerges. Read them like an oracle about the stories that have risen and fallen in the fire. And remember: this is the process. After the burning, the darkness, the ashes. All are necessary, all are blessed. The blood from your womb, the tears from your cheeks, the pain of the world and the ashes combine to make a prayer, which will fertilise new land. These ashes, this blood, this darkness, these tears are the earth of new dreams."

She stirs the ashes, watching intently. Then screams and jumps back as her finger hits a coal still glowing. All the women lean in, chins almost to the ground, and begin to blow, gently, gently.

As their breath joins the wind another woman begins to speak. "For me the blessing of Ashen Woman was the gift of 'no'.

"I remember when I used to say 'yes' when I meant 'no', and it caused me, and my partner and friends so much pain. In the end they were scared to ask me for anything, because I would be so angry. I would be stomping around, taking my frustration and tiredness out on them all.

"But burnout forced me to say the word I had been scared of, the word I had been avoiding. Suddenly I found myself having to say 'no', even when I wanted to say 'yes'. *No, sorry, I can't, I'm too sick, I'm too tired.* I found myself suddenly valuing my time and energy in a way I never had before. Previously I had said 'yes' to everything, scared of upsetting people, scared of missing out. But now my energy was limited I realised how precious it was.

"At first I hated letting people down. But after a while it became freeing, empowering. I, for the first time in my life, got to choose. I got to say what was important to me, and just do that. I got to dedicate myself to what I valued, rather than running myself ragged trying to be everything to everyone. And even though I had less energy than before, I realised I was more powerful. It took having the control taken away from me by my own body to actually take control of my own life.

"The problem is that as women we are trained to give more and more of ourselves away to others, we learn early on that we are never enough. We are rarely given permission to step away from things before they are done. Instead we wait until we are burned out before we start to seek permission to reign in our energy. I realised when I was sick, that it is up to us to give ourselves that permission. To determine our own enough, to decide when we can step back and trust the process. No one else is going to do it for us. They can support us in it, but we have to do it ourselves. We have to learn when we have given enough time, energy, thought, feeling to something, and that it is time to consciously disengage our energy. This doesn't mean that we stop feeling and shut down, that we abandon things or no longer care anymore, but it means that we consciously divert the majority of our energy flow towards ourselves and our Source energy in order to recharge. We have to learn that 'no' is just as rich and sacred, loving and valuable, as 'yes'."

A blonde woman nods, "I learned that I had to get really clear on receiving enough for what I did, it always felt so scary asking for what I wanted. In fact, half the time I didn't even know what I wanted, and so it was easier just not to say anything and take what I was given, even if it felt unfair, even if it wasn't enough to cover my energy or expenses. I guess it started when

I was a little girl, I was called greedy and it stuck. So instead I asked for nothing. Or I'd always give more than what I was paid for. And still I'd feel guilty. Until I found myself spreading my energy so thin, and living constantly on the verge of burnout. I felt ashamed.

"But I know it's not just me, I see it in my friends: the danger of over-giving and under-receiving is endemic. It's like we believe that we owe the world and that receiving — whether it's love, rest or money — just puts us more in debt. We have learned somehow to feel disempowered by receiving, and we gain some sort of power by giving. Sure it's a wonderful facet of women, giving without looking to receive, but it can get out of balance quickly, and means that we grab in secret, rather than ask for what we need. Learning to receive is a crucial part of the puzzle.

"We all know this feeling of our energy going in too many directions at once. Of feeling constantly drained. And it's making us sick."

The women nod in agreement. Knowing to the marrow of their bones the sense of exhaustion, the struggles they have experienced with receiving. Then a voice from the far side of the fire, her eyes made hollow in the firelight, shares her insight.

"I found that at times like that I need to reconnect with the power of gentle fire — not the fire that fuels our doing and our actions, but the one that soothes and nurtures my deep Feminine self. I know that I, like so many of us, get caught up in the need to burn bright, to do big — and then get that feeling of complete exhaustion. I become an empty pit of cold, dark sadness. This is when gentle fire is my friend: a hot bath, a log fire and a warm blanket, a gentle massage, my back against a heater, a hot water bottle on my belly, warm soup or a spicy curry with bread from the oven, a cup of tea and freshly baked cake with a dear friend. These are the things my mother used to do for me, when I was tired or sick or sad, and they never failed to soothe me and heal me. And so now I do them for myself. I guess a large part of really growing up is learning to mother ourselves."

"I need to try that," says the first woman, "I have had it pointed out to me that I put immense pressure on myself to be everything to everyone... and to do it perfectly. And I forget in the middle of it, that this incredible stuff I'm doing shouldn't just be for everyone else. I need to take the medicine of what moves through me, not just to give it all away. I need to step out of being the martyr, and nourish myself too. Because if I don't do this as a priority, I cannot burn. I can't do the work I'm here to do. It's been a hard learning curve, because we're not taught how to do this. I remember seeing my mother in tears at the end of each day, she was so tired, but she just couldn't stop. My father would be sitting reading the paper, and she'd always be on her feet tidying.

"He went and played golf with his friends, for half a day every weekend, but I never saw her go out with her friends. She didn't have a circle of women like this. She didn't have a life outside us children. And so I always thought that self-care was silly or selfish: I'd never seen her do it, so it was an alien concept when I first heard about it. But now I know that I need plenty of time to just be, and to trust my return to the stillness of the dark. And that if I don't go willingly to nurture myself in the dark, I will be dragged by my hair."

"That's right, my love," the poetess says softly, "to be able to inhabit our Feminine power we need to integrate self-care into the bedrock of our lives. It flies in the face of everything we have been taught, and the way that our world is built. We can think that our mission in this world should take priority over self-care. But don't you doubt it, self-care is a political act of inner defiance. It really is revolutionary. It marks a sea change. When we take care of ourselves, we honour the Feminine."

"These times of gentle fire, this taking care of ourselves," the woman on the far side of the fire continues, "teaches us another aspect of Burning Woman. We remember the power of an embodied touch or a word from the heart, holding space for another or simply holding them — these are other ways we embody the Feminine and bring it into the world. Ways that are so easy to forget, but matter so much. These are just as powerful as our works of art, our speeches and classes, our activism and daring. We need to weave the fierce and gentle aspects of Feminine fire together, through all of our lives."

The women's breath has roused the flames which begin to rise in the midst of the group once more, casting their shadows onto the trees behind them. Shadows far bigger and more menacing than the women themselves.

"I so love hearing about the gentleness," a small woman with a long shadow said. "But then I start to feel angry, because it's not all gentleness. We sit together in these circles and call each other sisters and just seem to conveniently forget what utter bitches women can be."

The silence in the circle deepens, a fiery energy is tangible. Something has arisen that wasn't there before. Sparks shower from the fire, and the women instinctively move back from it. "I mean, it's all very well talking about the nice stuff, but it makes me want to scream. Why do we never talk about the dark side of power? The twisted shadow of sisterhood. The way we burn each other. The way we make each other spark. It's like we feel we are being disloyal to our so-called sisters if we tell the truth about it.

"There's so much darkness, anger, attacking and hurt by women, on women everywhere I go. I'm scared to write on my blog nowadays for fear of being trolled, I saw it happen to my best friend and it just destroyed her. They took her apart and burned her alive, like a lynch mob, it was horrible. It reminded me of the mean girls in the school playground, only now they're all grown up. And they cause real damage. But no one's talking about it. It's trivialised and portrayed as just bitch fights, silly women's stuff. But it's not trivial, it's having a massive impact on us all. . . and on our world. It shuts us down. Stops us doing our thing. Speaking our truths. Showing up. This darkness is keeping us small. Why don't we talk about it?"

The question hangs in the chill night air. The women shift in their seats.

"I know I don't talk about it," another woman begins, "because I feel ashamed. It's like I know I'm part of the dance. But I can't see how to deal with it. One of my biggest struggles as someone who identifies strongly as a Burning Woman, is how to burn alongside others. It's what I long to do. . . but it comes with massive dangers. I haven't found a way to burn safely together, and so I tend to burn alone. It makes me feel sad and angry and lonely quite often, but it's safer this way. Each time I try to share leadership, each time I am involved in a group, it all seems to be going well, but I'm on my guard, making sure I'm not stepping on anyone's toes. I gain confidence, I start sharing the deeper layers of myself, becoming more vocal, trying hard to burn true to myself and not overwhelm others. And then suddenly, it's like a box of fireworks has gone off. There's hurt breaking out everywhere, and it's my fault. I seem to have started it, even though I was trying to be so careful. And so I slink away, or more often burn that bridge and hide at home, overwhelmed with hurt, with being misunderstood. It's like in the choice between being true to myself and sharing power with others, someone always gets hurt. And I hate hurt."

The blonde woman joins in, "I've seen it happen so many times, when two women of fire work closely together, we become like fiery hedgehogs. Whilst we're sparking off each other and agreeing with each other, it's exciting, productive and we feel so heartened by the sisterhood. But it only takes one wrong word, one misstep, just a simple disagreement on something trivial and our soft bellies are wounded by the spikes of the other. I hate that feeling so much. It goes from nice to nuclear in a moment and there's this sense of deep shock: just a moment ago all was great, and now it's all gone up in flames. There's this overwhelming desire to be able to put the genie back in the bottle, to unsay the words, unfeel the feeling, but it's so big and all-consuming and upsetting.

"I wish there was a way that we didn't upset each other like that. I wish there was a way we could share our truths with each other without this massive triggering. It's like we have two settings: nice, friendly and superficial. Or raw, real, and nuclear. It happens again and again, between mothers and daughters, best friends, creative collaborators. We say we want honesty, depth and truth, but we can't take it, no matter how tactfully it is shared. Suddenly our sister has turned from ally to attacker. It takes a strong willingness to turn it round from there. Mostly we get blasted apart by these experiences. We burn our bridges, walk away. And have our fingers burned from attempting any future intimacy with that woman. . . or any other woman for that matter.

"And it's a woman thing. I just don't see it in the men in my life. Not that degree of sensitivity. . . or fallout. We know these energy dynamics as women, but most of us still have not found how to work through them, within ourselves, or between each other."

"Thank you for having the courage to mention this," another voice says, that has remained silent until now. Her voice shakes in powerful emotion, tears streaming down her face. "This is really raw for me. I was burned badly. When I least expected it, by someone dear to me. Someone I thought of as a sister. It seemed to come out of nowhere, everything was fine, just normal, we were working together on a project, and then she just turned on me. It was as though something had been unleashed, I was shocked and hurt. And I kept reminding myself, *It's not personal*, but it feels that way at the time. And it just drained all the energy out of me."

The women around the fire nod, recognising the experience of standing in their vulnerability, inhabiting their power and being burned by other women.

The woman continues, "It seems that some dark stuff gets released once we start to do this women's work. And it lashes out at the most powerful person in the room, like lightning going to ground. It's scary but I think it's part of this burning stuff. . . it's got to be. It's so common, this pattern of behaviour. We come together, make something great and we feel good and then at the height of the process it's like a fiery venom is unleashed. Then almost as suddenly it came, it clears. . . but leaving scorch marks on its path and relationships torn asunder.

"It seems that something bigger is at play, some larger, more universal power dynamic. This energy, the energy of Burning Woman that we are working with is a thing, it has its own unique properties and patterns, that we have not been initiated into. And because most of us are venturing into it alone, uninitiated by those who have walked this path before us, we are unprepared for the consequences.

"When that shadow power rises up it's really scary. Because it doesn't care about boundaries, it just wants to burn everything down. It's terrifying, so we make our lives revolve around staying small and safe and avoiding conflict.

"When it happened to me I was so scared, it felt like my whole world was falling down. It was like being stung by a scorpion, the feeling of her barbs, lodged like glass in my guts. I was so ashamed, so I kept it to myself, but it began to eat me alive. It took all my courage to speak openly about the situation for the first time. But I found, when I did, lots of women started to step out of the shadows and say, *Me too.*"

The poetess leans forward, and looks each of the women in the eye. "You are not alone. We must remind ourselves, precious ones, when a woman's shadow side comes after us — it's NOT personal.

"She will make it personal, using names, and words that she knows will cut. Because that is, in her mind, what has provoked her fury. But the power you are feeling from her is her own shadow power which she dares not unleash in the way she sees you do it. So she criticises you, and the way you do it, because of her own inner critics, her own frustrations. Her words do not define you. They cannot. This is the shadow power of Burning Woman unleashed. It is not personal.

"It hurts most when those who burn you are those you believe to be your allies, they burn you with their words, because they're too scared to put their power into their own burning. They're too scared to join you naked in the fire, so they throw fire bombs from a safe distance.

"Take it as validation. The sparks from another's fire have been awoken by your own. But she does not yet know how to transmute this energy, and so it gets twisted and black as it pushes past her blockages to be released.

"Step aside and let the sparks fall to the ground and die out, or they will seed your own fire. If your critics are interested in helping you grow, in constructive rather than destructive criticism, they will dare to get naked with you and dance in the fire together in mutual vulnerability. They will talk with you, rather than throwing fire and running for cover, and gathering a mob. We have to own our own power first, and our shadow power, before we can stand in true sisterhood. We are learning."

"We need to learn how to handle conflict like mature women," a woman with flame red hair says, "We fight like girls at the moment. Trying to destroy each other, being in petty competition. Once we stand in our own power, we don't need to worry about anyone taking it away, because they can't: it's internal. We don't need to assert our authority or worry about anyone disrespecting it. We know we can draw our own boundaries, rather than defences.

"We need to learn how to disagree, to have healthy differences of opinion, to hold space for them to co-exist. We still believe that difference is wrong and that disapproval will kill us. For most of history being female has been a competition for survival and we've come to believe that we're so fragile that a conflict could shatter us into a thousand pieces. But it won't. We can be together but different. There is enough power for us all. There is enough. We don't need to believe their lies of scarcity any more.

"We've all watched our mothers and grandmothers deal with conflict in the only ways they knew. From them we have learned to burn bridges, smoulder in passive aggression, scream like a banshee or become a martyr. And these are the same patterns we bring out into all our relationships, and conflicts in the world.

"Most of us have learned to see conflict as war: a violent, destructive, unhealthy part of the masculine realm which terrifies us. But conflict is a part of life, it reflects the paradox of existence and how complexity can exist. Once we are aware of our power and its shadow, when we are aware of our defence structures, when we realise that neither of us is in mortal danger, then we can become curious about conflict as a way towards resolution and a fuller life, rather than defending ourselves from death. We don't need to be scared of it.

"I believe that the tension between two women in power can be a beautiful symphony when both are secure in their own authority and selves. How we treat each other in the midst of the storm, how we allow space for the wounded self, the old stories and archetypes, how we choose to hold space and find healing together, rather than act defensively is an act of maturity that we are still learning."

"It was Eve Ensler that really made this clear for me," the hollow eyed woman adds. "She said, 'To be truly powerful, you have to get to the place where you can tolerate people not liking you.' I couldn't tolerate that for a long, long time. Other women's disapproval felt like death for me. I spent my life apologising for everything. I felt like I was apologising for my very existence. Every criticism was confirmation of my inner belief that there was something wrong with me. I needed to be approved of just to survive. I was in constant inner conflict, second-guessing myself, looking for approval, to know I was doing things right. But her words lit a spark in me. How could I tolerate the disapproval of others? I've had to live into that question.

"What I learned was that I had to settle deep into my bones and listen for my own answers first, rather than racing around looking for everyone else's opinions about what I should do and who I should be. It was really hard at first, because when I did that, I realised that I could screw up. I could be disliked for what I did: people might turn against me or criticise me. But then two words suddenly hit me: *so what?* They would disapprove. . . and I would live. Their criticism would not, could not, kill me. The world would keep on turning. In that moment I realised that I had the right to do my work in my way. No one else could take it away.

"When I was younger, everyone else's authority trumped my own. I felt like there was 'right' and 'wrong', and if it wasn't 'right' in someone else's eyes, then it must be, or rather, I must be, 'wrong'. But as I've walked this path, I've realised it's more nuanced than that, and that I will never please all of the people, all of the time. And that whilst my work is here to serve others, it is not at the expense of my commitment to my Source, or to myself. I cannot, must not sacrifice myself on the altar of other's demands. Then I began to have the courage to truly live into the wisdom of Burning Woman."

The poetess stands to close the circle. The silver in her hair reflecting the fire light.

"Oh sisters, I am blessed by your stories,

By the presence of both your light and your shadow.

By your strength and vulnerability.

Let us root ourselves in them.

Now is the time to learn to stand together in our differences.

Now is the time to embody our own authority.

Now is the time to move away from the shackles of perfection and towards ever-evolving co-creativity.

Now is the time to learn the power of our 'yes' and our 'no', and use each wisely.

Now is the time to know ourselves as fierce and gentle.

Now is the time to inhabit paradox as our holy temple.

Now is the time, sisters.

Now is the time.

So step up, step into the fire.

Let her claim you as her own

Let yourself be transformed in the burning.

It is time, Burning Women,

Arise!"

12

DANCING IN THE FLAMES

A Flock of Phoenix

We don't have to know how to do it.
We just have to know we want to do it.
This is the time when women and work
rise together.
A Phoenix adorned in fire red and diamonds,
ready to fly to her next destination. . .

A new chapter is being written.
A new prophecy is being called out.
Women are wise. Women are wealthy. . .

We, who are able, must rise.
And make space for others to rise.
Each of us makes up her own fire rising song.

We sing the words into creation.
And watch the sparks begin to fly.
Just because fire was used against us
does not mean we gave up fire.

No. We have breathed fire, taken it into our being.

Our legend is not only one of burning.
But one of knowing fire!
Our legend is one of rising. Of flying.
Of making the impossible flight from ashes.

Dusting the gray from our fire red wings, we extend our
shimmering wings.

And the Earth in her wisdom pushes us from beneath.
And the air in her understanding pulls us from above.

Up we go. Free at last.
Leaving gravity to its daily chore
of holding all things in place.
But not us. Not today.
Today, we soar and we are whole.
We find the sky full of radiant Phoenix.
A whole flock of Phoenix Women.
And together, we fly on the wisdom
of the shared flock.
Bright and beautiful. Bold and dangerous.
Wild and full of hope. Brave and abundant.
Let us rise oh Winged Sisters and claim our skies!

Shiloh Sophia McCloud

A CULTURE ON FIRE

*These are not comforting times in which to make promises; the stakes
are too high, we are playing with forms of death from which there
may be no return, and all the endings are still uncertain.*

We can only begin.

*Take hands; for we are the circle of rebirth. If there is to be renewal,
it begins with us. . . We can know the dark, and dream it into a new
image.*
Starhawk, *Dreaming the Dark*

Our nostrils twitch, smelling burning. But this time, this time
it is not us on the pyre. Not our bodies. It is our Earth. The
way of patriarchal power has bound and raped and burned
her. Her temperature is rising, she is quaking and shaking,
she is storming. She is exhibiting all the signs we know of
transformation. We can ignore her and die with her, or stand
for and transform with her.

The world is burning.

As I finish writing this book, a great tract of Earth is on fire in
Indonesia and threatened species are being driven out of their
habitats.

This has been a year of burning.

According to The Washington Post, the summer of 2015 was
the worst wildfire season in Alaska. Ever. Out of control fires
ravaged 11 million acres in Canada and Alaska transforming
the permafrost ground beneath. [xxxiv]

There is a phrase—"fire weather"—which refers to excessively
dry conditions which are conducive to wildfires. On a global
environmental scale, fire weather is increasing.

But it is not just our environment. Tensions are rising, as
acts of brutality mount — massacres in Paris, Beirut, Belgium,
Tunisia, all over Syria and Iraq. Daylight kidnappings of women

and girls in Nigeria and Mexico, almost-daily mass shootings in the US. On a human level we are reaching boiling point.

The scale of the atrocities, frustrations on a global scale, the stress levels and lack of support in our personal lives are creating perfect conditions for wildfire. We are drying out and cracking under the heat and strain — the life-giving waters that could keep us moist and flowing are diverting underground, or being polluted. And so a single spark can set us ablaze —outrage can erupt at any moment, threatening death and destruction.

The anguish is real. It is so deeply painful to look at the world around us and feel the volume of suffering that is happening on a daily basis.

We hardly dare trust that this is a process of transformation —that out of the ashes will rise the phoenix of humanity.

The Dalai Lama says that the world will be saved by Western women. And you and I know that at the forefront will be Burning Woman —running on a different power source to the world which is falling into flames around her. She has already disentangled herself from the wreckage of the patriarchal culture, so she will not be dazed, confused and disorientated by the systemic changes happening around her. Centred within herself, receptive to the Earth beyond her, she knows how to cultivate from the ashes, she knows how to find the embers to fuel the new fire.

Our time is now.

Our time has come.

For centuries and more they hunted you down, used you and punished you for your beauty, truth and your magical mystery. Suddenly, they seem to simply ask for it. They don't fear you. They beg and plead for you to help them. They once called you a witch, chained you down, burnt you and tossed you down a cliff to see if you would fly. Now you do and there they are, watching you in awe as you rise like a phoenix from the ashes of their primeval cursed fires.

All along they blamed you for witchcraft and black magic when all along it was them who used the dark forces to torture your bright soul. Your body and mind may have died over and over but your spirit persisted and here you are again, blooming, as bright as ever. The courage you have had over lifetimes is ineffable, beyond grasping and spectacularly baffling. You have withstood so much and yet you have kept coming back. You have trusted defeat to be the beginning of victory and therefore you have been resilient. Your strength is unlike many. The memories of your past battles stretching far back in history of mankind are imprinted in your body and today you can honor them. Today you can reveal yourself and give thanks to the courage you have showed over lifetimes. You have fought long and hard and are beginning to see that you can finally put your sword down, knowing that you mustn't always be on guard. You have made it safely to this point in time and space and here you can finally reside in peace. You were a warrior, a princess with a blade sharpened by love. You were a healer, a goddess with hands of light. You were a speaker with a quick tongue perfected for wisdoms of the heart. Now you are all those things you ever were, just not chased and imprisoned for it. Now you are a free bird, wings spreading high and wide.

Antonia Rothschild

TRAIL-BLAZING

We are crossing the demilitarized zone, the no-fly zone, as we navigate the transition from disempowerment to full throttle engagement as women burning a line of sand through the heart of a new landscape. Be aware that there will be retaliation. . . but find the strength through sisterhood and your own stately soul to not be sucked back into the victimhood of the old paradigm. Together, we build the new Temple from within.

Barbara Hill, writer, NYC

The fire will not die down again.

Not on our watch.

It is time, it is time,

For the fire of life to meet the Earth and her people.

It is time for the fire of the Feminine to infuse every aspect of our beings.

What lies unspoken must be spoken,

The silent must be heard,

The old offered up as sacrifice so its shells might be blown apart with new life,

Cracked through with new beginnings.

It is time, it is time,

The clocks are changing

The old stories are dead.

It is time, it is time,

Oh Kali come,

Sword flaming

Unbinding our bellies

And let us breathe our first breaths in a new land.

Free up our ribs,

Make them our own

And then we have the strength to breathe the embers into flames.

It is time to be free from the chains of old power

How have they held us this long?

We can no longer believe their stories,

When we have felt the truth in our own bodies.

The storm winds shake them to their foundations

And the fire burns through.

It is time to let go of the shore and ride the tails of the storm winds

into the fire.

It is time to rip the history books to shreds,

And write new stories, paint new pictures.

Dare you set the truth free from your own tongue?

It is time.

Are you ready?

We are free.

We are so used to women being an inconsequential part of history. But Burning Women have always appeared, and the more who burn, the more that will fill the pages of the books of our granddaughters and great-granddaughters. Imagine the our-story books of the future: we are writing them today through our lives.

Often we can get caught in our own struggles, our own small stories, and we forget our place in the larger story arc — the way that our actions, our choices, our achievements can and will blaze trails for those who come after us, so that they do not have to spend their time and energy re-fighting the same battles. It is time to know for sure that we can heal and release the old patterns that have kept the women of our Motherlines trapped.

We walk a spiral path, but for generations of women the spirals were so tightly packed that it seemed they were going round in circles — let us blaze trails so that the path we walk takes in wider and wider sweeps of human experience.

Trail blazing is what we do when we find ourselves in the wilderness, with no map and no path to guide us but our own intuitive understanding of nature and our destination. It is a forgotten skill. We push aside branches, or cut them back, we tramp down nettles and long grasses, ford rivers and streams, through inner and outer landscapes. We push the undergrowth back not just for ourselves, but for those who come after.

At times we must walk through the night, guided only by the stars. We know when to sit and rest, and when to strike on. We know where it is safe to gather water or set the campfire. We know what on the trail will sustain us and what will do us harm. We are courageous and cautious in equal measure. We are driven forward not only by our own desire to reach our destination, but also by the desire to leave a visible way for others who follow.

As we blaze forwards let us hold this advice from Rainer Maria Rilke like a talisman.

Be patient toward all that is unsolved in your heart and try to love the questions themselves. Do not now seek the answers, which cannot be given you because you would not be able to live them. Live everything. Live the questions now. Perhaps you will then gradually, without noticing it, live along some distant day into the answer.

My hope for you is that as our time together here finishes that you are filled not with answers, but questions.

Burning questions.

Questions that will set you alight from the inside. Questions you can spend your life living into as you blaze new trails into this burning world.

Allow the questions to illuminate your life, live into them in open curiosity, rather than replace one set of one-dimensional answers with another, exchanging one prison for another.

The Burning Woman stands with one foot and her head in the old world, the world of separation, and one foot and her heart in the new world. Burning Woman is she who bridges the gap, in the words of Charles Eisenstein, to "the more beautiful world our hearts know is possible".

Fire lights her up from the inside, it lights the darkness for others, and it burns through the old, the dead and the dying, the last vestiges of a culture which no longer serves us.

Burning Women stand strong.

Burning Woman show us the way.

I am, you are, a vital cell in the awakening Feminine on Earth, a crucial component in consciousness realizing itself in form. You, your experience, is not insignificant, it is part of a larger awakening of the Feminine incarnate.

Nature is calling the women, and we hear her birth cries.

Around the world women are gathering in red tents, in women's circles, in meetings and online. We are circling.

These are burning times. And they call for Burning Women. Women embodying their passion. Women feeling in their bodies. Creative women. Courageous women. Connected women.

Gather the women. Gather the men. Let Burning Women and Burning Men come together in ecstatic creative partnership. In dangerous acts of creative rebellion.

Rip your clothes off, run towards the flames and dance like there's no tomorrow to the beat of your own heart. Only you can hear the rhythm, only you know its tune, only your body can dance this way, so do it. Stop holding back, and waiting, and trying to do it right, and not upset anyone.

I am there right beside you. I see your courage, I sense your power, I hear your voice. You are not alone.

We are ready. We hold the torches, we circle. We are the carriers of life-giving flames. We burn from the inside. The Feminine inflammation, a conflagration of sisters, burning away the bitter past and lighting the way to the future.

It is time.

Will you join us?

We often fear that the Revolution needed is too big for what we can give.

Too much change is required inside, outside.

And we are too small.

But all that is required is that you step into the truth of your life.

And speak it, write it, paint it, dance it.

That you shine your light on your truth, for the world to see.

And as hundreds, then thousands, then millions do this—each sparking the courage of yet more—

Suddenly we have a world alight with truth.

We are shifting ourselves.

We are shifting the world.

Dancing her into a new orbit.

We are filling in the space where our voices were silenced

Filling in the blanks where our images have been lacking.

We are weaving her-story into reality.

Unweaving the limiting his-stories.

Creating our-story.

Reaching beyond religion and patriarchy and capitalism and so-called democracy

Into new ways of being and seeing.

We are the bridge between worlds

We are the ones we have been waiting for.

Arise, Burning Woman!

Arise, Burning Women!

AFTERWORD

The visionary is the one who brings her voice into the world and who refuses to edit, rehearse, perform, or hide. It is the visionary who knows that the power of creativity is aligned with authenticity.

Angeles Arrien

Each book I write brings with it a shift for me, a journey I need to take. When I accept the invitation to write, I know that I am accepting the invitation to wonder and wander into the unknown and take notes on the process. This is my commitment to me, and to you. Each time it scares me and thrills me in almost equal measure, because the path will require that I unturn what has lain hidden, unblock what has lain blocked, and see what I have refused.

Each time it breaks me open. It takes me to the far reaches of my comfort zone and beyond, challenging me in ways I have previously shrunk from.

I am deeply grateful for the gift.

But, my goddess, is it scary.

I started this book with fire in my belly. But as I wrote, I moved into the safer terrain of my mind. I wanted to give you the answers to how to be a Burning Woman and create the comprehensive step-by-step guide. I felt the urge to help save the women of the world before lunch time once again. I felt the duty of obligation on my shoulders. It got heavier and heavier. And as I tried to plough through I got more and more bogged down, bored, frustrated and resentful. Despite the fact that I was writing about following your own pleasure as a Burning Woman, I was not following mine. The last laugh was on me as I followed my Good Girl script whilst writing about how to burn it. But all the time questioning my own expertise and authority to do so.

When I was stuck, deeply entrenched, nothing was flowing and all was darkness, I realised I needed to take my own advice. When something's not working, despite trying and trying, stop trying, let go. Sit in the darkness. Set fire to it all, watch it go up in flames, and see where the smoke leads you. And so tens of thousands of words were discarded, the book was stripped bare until only bones remained.

Burning Woman has held big and powerful medicine for me. Its birthing process has been strong, Littered often with nightmares and despair. But also with sisterhood and hope. And breakthroughs galore. It has burned away so much of the old, leaving me a clearer vista, where I can feel my inner spark, touch my creative river flowing once more. It sparked another powerful new book that I have dived straight into, and can't wait to share *Medicine Woman* with you very soon.

Through writing this book I have discovered that I can do what I never thought I had the courage to do. And live to tell the tale. What power and peace we have, when we lay down the battle with ourselves, when we quit holding our soul's toes to the fire, and instead allow ourselves to enter the darkness, open to our inner flame and shoot to life. When we lay down our battle with our loved ones and find ways to creatively engage in reweaving the world.

This is what I wish for you, and for myself.

Here's to us, Burning Women, as we blaze bright trails through the dark.

Lucy Pearce, Shanagarry, Ireland. January 2016.

END NOTES

i.   The Washington Post-Kaiser Foundation 2014

ii.   http://www.guide2womenleaders.com/Current-Women-Leaders.htm

iii.   http://money.cnn.com/2015/03/24/investing/female-ceo-pipeline-leadership/

iv.   http://money.cnn.com/2015/01/13/news/companies/women-corporate-board-global/index.html

v.   Fawcett Report

vi.   Guerrilla Girls http://www.guerrillagirls.com/posters/venicewallf.shtml

vii.   https://en.wikipedia.org/wiki/Patriarchy

viii.   William Monter: "Witch trials in Continental Europe" in *Witchcraft and Magic in Europe*, ed. Bengst Ankarloo & Stuart Clark, University of Pennsylvania Press, Philadelphia 2002

ix.   Pavlac, Brian A. "Ten Common Errors and Myths about the Witch Hunts, Corrected and Commented," Prof. Pavlac's Women's History Resource Site (2 May 2012). http://departments.kings.edu/womens_history/witcherrors.html

x.   Gibson, M (2006). "Witchcraft in the Courts" in Gibson, Marion. *Witchcraft and Society in England And America, 1550–1750.*

xi.   *The Esoteric Codex: Witch Hunting*, Samuel Covington

xii.   *Caliban and the Witch*

xiii.   *Caliban and the Witch*

xiv.   Thurston, 2001

xv.   *History of Fentress County, Tennessee*, Albert R. Hogue, compiled by the Fentress County Historical Society

xvi.   Ally, Yaseen (June 2009). "Witch Hunts in Modern South Africa"

xvii.   "World Report on Violence and Health" (PDF), World Health Organization

xviii. www.bbc.com/news/magazine-19437130

xix. www.theatlantic.com/international/archive/2013/08/saudi-arabias-war-on-witchcraft/278701

xx. Mezzofiore, Gianluca (June 30, 2015). "Isis in Syria: Islamic State beheads 2 women for sorcery reports Syrian Observatory for Human Rights", *International Business Times*

xxi. http://www.who.int/mental_health/prevention/genderwomen/en/

xxii. http://www.theguardian.com/science/2015/aug/21/study-of-holocaust-survivors-finds-trauma-passed-on-to-childrens-genes

xxiii. World Food Program.org, Women and Hunger

xxiv. http://www.nber.org/papers/w15041

xxv. World Bank, 2006

xxvi. http://www.un.org/esa/gopher-data/conf/fwcw/conf/una/950906150325.txt

xxvii. Study conducted by University of North Carolina at Chapel Hill, 2008 in association with Self magazine. http://www.sciencedaily.com/releases/2008/04/080422202514.htm

xxviii. Carlat, D.J., Camargo. "Review of Bulimia Nervosa in Males" American Journal of Psychiatry, 154, 1997.

xxix. "Characteristics and Treatment of Patients with Chronic Eating Disorders", by Dr. Greta Noordenbox, International Journal of Eating Disorders, Volume 10: 15-29, 2002.

xxx. Shisslak, C.M., Crago, M., & Estes, L.S. (1995). "The Spectrum of Eating Disturbances" International Journal of Eating Disorders, 18 (3): 209-219.

xxxi. Wade, T. D., Keski-Rahkonen A., & Hudson J. "Epidemiology of Eating Disorders" in M. Tsuang and M. Tohen (Eds.), *Textbook in Psychiatric Epidemiology* (3rd ed.). New York: Wiley, 2011. p. 343-360.

xxxii. Mayo Clinic, 2014.

xxxiii. *The Uterine Companion*, Dr Eve Agee

xxxiv. http://www.washingtonpost.com/news/energy-environment/wp/2015/07/26/alaskas-terrifying-wildfire-season-and-what-it-says-about-climate-change/

RESOURCES

THE FEMININE

The Heart of the Labyrinth, Nicole Schwab

The Other Side of the River: Stories of Women, Water and the World, Eila Kundrie Carrico

Red, Hot and Holy, Sera Beak

Dreaming the Dark: Magic, Sex and Politics, Starhawk

Waking Up to the Dark: Ancient Wisdom for Sleepless Times, Clark Strand

Longing for Darkness: Tara and the Black Madonna, China Galland

Untie the Strong Woman: Blessed Mother's Immaculate Love for the Wild Soul, Clarissa Pinkola Estés

Journey to the Dark Goddess: How to Return to Your Soul, Jane Meredith

Kissing the Hag: The Dark Goddess and the Unacceptable Nature of Women, Emma Restall-Orr

Body of Wisdom: Women's Spiritual Power and How it Serves, Hilary Hart

Shakti Woman: Feeling Our Fire, Healing our World, Vicki Noble

PaGaian Cosmology: Re-inventing Earth-Based Goddess Religion, Glenys Livingstone

ARCHETYPE, METAPHOR AND SYMBOL

The Red Book, C.G. Jung

The Archetypes and The Collective Unconscious (Collected Works of C.G. Jung Vol.9 Part 1), C. G. Jung

Word and Image, C. G. Jung and Aniela Jaffé

Archetypes: A Beginner's Guide to Your Inner-net, Caroline Myss

Sacred Contracts: Awakening Your Divine Potential, Caroline Myss

The Heroines Journey, Maureen Murdock

The Power of Myth, Joseph Campbell

The Hero with a Thousand Faces, Joseph Campbell

The Uses of Enchantment: The Meaning and Importance of Fairy Tales, Bruno Bettelheim

Kiss Sleeping Beauty Goodbye: Breaking the Myth of Feminine Myths and Models, Madonna Kolbenschlag

Language and the Transformation of Consciousness, Julia Penelope

Speaking Freely: Unlearning the Lies of the Fathers' Tongues, Julia Penelope

Gyn/Ecology: The Metaethics of Radical Feminism, Mary Daly

Dancing in the Flames: The Dark Goddess in the Transformation of Consciousness, Marion Woodman and Elinor Dickson

A Field Guide to Getting Lost, Rebecca Solnit

The Shadow King: Ending the Tyranny of the Inner Patriarch, Sidra Stone

The Witch and the Clown: Two Archetypes of Human Sexuality, Barry and Ann Ulanov

Women Who Run with the Wolves: Myths and Stories of the Wild Woman Archetype, Clarissa Pinkola Estés

The Rainbow Way: Cultivating Creativity in the Midst of Motherhood, Lucy H. Pearce

PATRIARCHY, FEMINISM AND WOMEN'S HISTORY

The Heroine's Club: A Mother-Daughter Empowerment Circle, Melia Keeton-Digby

Caliban and the Witch: Women, the Body and Primitive Accumulation, Silvia Federici

Witch-Hunting, Past and Present, and the Fear of the Power of Women, Silvia Federici

Witchcraze: A New History of the European Witch Hunts: Our Legacy of Violence Against Women, Anne Barstow

Witchhunts in the Western World, Brian A. Pavlac

Demon Lover, The Roots of Terrorism, Robin Morgan

But She Said: Feminist Practices of Biblical Interpretation, Elisabeth Schüssler Fiorenza

The Second Sex, Elizabeth Gould Davis

Not in His Image, John Lamb Lash

Intercourse, Andrea Dworkin

Life and Death. Unapologetic Writings on the Continuing War Against Women, Andrea Dworkin

Woman Hating, Andrea Dworkin

The Dance of the Dissident Daughter, Sue Monk Kidd

Stupid White Men:. . . And Other Sorry Excuses for the State of the Nation, Michael Moore

Gyn/Ecology: The Metaethics of Radical Feminism, Mary Daly

Men Explain Things to Me, Rebecca Solnit

The Female Eunuch, Germaine Greer

Fat is a Feminist Issue, Susie Orbach

The Feminine Mystique, Betty Friedan

The Beauty Myth: How Images of Beauty Are Used Against Women, Naomi Wolf

The Twisted Sisterhood: Unraveling the Fall Out of Aggression Among Girls and Women, Pushing for a More Mindful Civility, Kelly Valen

Cunt: A Declaration of Independence, Inga Muscio

Sister Outsider: Essays and Speeches, Audre Lorde

Women and Honor: Some Notes on Lying, Adrienne Rich

The Trouble with Women, Jackie Fleming

Feminism is for Everyone, bell hooks

The Chalice and the Blade. Our History, Our Future, Riane Eisler

NEW PARADIGM

The More Beautiful World our Hearts Know is Possible, Charles Eisenstein

A New Earth: Awakening to Your Life's Purpose, Eckhart Tolle

The Aquarian Conspiracy: Personal and Social Transformation in our Time, Marilyn Ferguson

Women, Spirituality and Transformative Leadership: Where Grace Meets Power, Kathe Schaaf and Kay Lindahl

MOTHER

The Motherline, Naomi Lowinsky

My Mother, Myself, Nancy Friday

Moods of Motherhood: The Inner Journey of Mothering,
Lucy H. Pearce

Healing the Mother Wound, e-course at WombofLight.com

OXYTOCIN, ADRENALIN AND TRAUMA

The Oxytocin Factor, Kerstin Moberg

Childbirth in the Age of Plastic, Michel Odent

A Secure Base: Parent-Child Attachment and Healthy Human Development, John Bowlby

The Highly Sensitive Person: How to Thrive When the World Overwhelms You, Elaine Aron

In an Unspoken Voice: How the Body Releases Trauma and Restores Goodness, Peter A. Levine

Trauma and Memory: Brain and Body in a Search for the Living Past: A Practical Guide for Understanding and Working with Traumatic Memory, Peter A. Levine

The Shock Doctrine: The Rise of Disaster Capitalism,
Naomi Klein

E-courses at Irene Lyon

ENERGY, POWER AND BOUNDARIES

Energy Anatomy: The Science of Personal Power, Spirituality and Health, Caroline Myss (audio)

Anatomy of the Spirit: The Seven Stages of Power and Healing, Caroline Myss

Hands of Light: A Guide to Healing Through the Human Energy Field, Barbara Ann Brennan

Eastern Body, Western Mind: Psychology and the Chakra System as a Path to the Self, Anodea Judith

Energy Medicine for Women: Aligning Your Body's Energies to Boost Your Health and Vitality, Donna Eden

Energetic Boundaries: How to Stay Protected and Connected in Work, Love, and Life, Cyndi Dale

Maps to Ecstasy: The Healing Power of Movement, Gabrielle Roth

Kundalini: Divine Energy, Divine Life, Cyndi Dale

Mountain Lion, e-course at PixieLighthorse.com

Coming Alive! Rebecka Eggers

HEALING MIND AND BODY

The Gifts of Imperfection: Let Go of Who You Think You're Supposed to Be and Embrace Who You Are, Brené Brown

Daring Greatly: How the Courage to Be Vulnerable Transforms the Way We Live, Love, Parent, and Lead, Brené Brown

I Thought It Was Just Me: Women Reclaiming Power and Courage in a Culture of Shame, Brené Brown

Wild Soul: Igniting Your Passion and Potential in Work, Home and Life, Tami Lynn Kent

Wild Feminine: Finding Power, Spirit and Joy in the Female Body, Tami Lynn Kent

The Female Brain, Louann Brizendine

Sexual Practices of the Quodoshka: Teachings from the Nagual Tradition, Amara Charles

Burnout to Brilliance: Strategies for Sustainable Success, Jayne Morris

Art is a Way of Knowing, Pat B. Allen

Art is a Spiritual Path, Pat B. Allen

Letting in the Wild Edges, Glennie Kindred

Madness and Civilization, Foucault

The Spiritual Gift of Madness: The Failure of Psychiatry and the Rise of the Mad Pride Movement, Seth Farber

Spiritual Emergency, Stanislav Grof

MENSTRUAL CYCLE

Moon Time: Harness the Ever-changing Energy of Your Menstrual Cycle, Lucy H. Pearce

Alchemy for Women: Personal Transformation Through Dreams and the Female Cycle, Penelope Shuttle and Peter Redgrove

The Wise Wound: Menstruation and Every Woman, Penelope Shuttle and Peter Redgrove

Red Moon: Understanding and Using the Creative, Sexual and Spiritual Gifts of the Menstrual Cycle, Miranda Gray

The Wild Genie: The Healing Power of Menstruation, Alexandra Pope

The Uterine Companion: A Holistic Guide to Life-Long Wellness, Dr Eve Agee

BURNING WOMAN PLAY LIST

Starting with soothing power songs to ignite the fire within, and finishing with some rebel rousing tunes to start a revolution!

Leah Song and Nahko Bear by firelight on the beach
https://youtu.be/O7J0MhVj_2E

Rising Appalachia
Medicine https://youtu.be/czkHmjrFCnM
Scale Down https://youtu.be/Bmr5rdaemYk

Medicine for the People
Risk It https://youtu.be/4g_RLzf9oiU
Black as Night https://youtu.be/lkGBLLjAXEA

Peruquois: Earth Woman, Priestess
https://youtu.be/r56D5J_HiNE

Christy Moore
The Burning Times https://youtu.be/RntnpYTfpSc

CopperWoman *Blessingway*

ALisa Starkweather *Daughter of the Earth*

The Prodigy *Firestarter*

Patti Smith *Wild Horses*

BURNING WOMAN FILM RESOURCES

Suffragette

Frida

Hysteria

The Goddess Project http://thegoddessproject.com

Also check out their short film *Shine*
http://www.thegoddessproject.com/shine

Things We Don't Talk About—Narratives from the Red Tent

Capitalism: A love story

COURSES

This is a list of brave Burning Souls whose work has hugely helped me and others. I trust and endorse them as authentic soul workers on the cutting edge of healing and connecting people to their authentic power. They know. . . because they've done it themselves.

Pixie Lighthorse pixielighthorse.com

Bethany Webster womboflight.com

Charles Eisenstein charleseisenstein.net

Shiloh Sophia shilohsophiastudios.com

Flora Bowley florabowley.com

Birthing Ourselves into Being
BirthingOurselvesintoBeing.com

Irene Lyon irenelyon.com

Hali Karla halikarla.com

Brené Brown Power of Vulnerability course on Udemy.com

WEB REFERENCES

http://www.huffingtonpost.com/jenny-g-perry/love-a-wild-one_b_4352714.html

http://www.wakingtimes.com/2014/08/22/shaman-sees-mental-hospital/

http://endofcapitalism.com/2009/11/05/who-were-the-witches-patriarchal-terror-and-the-creation-of-capitalism/

http://beingpresenthealing.com/2015/10/16/suffragette-the-journey-must-continue/

http://taprootdoula.com/2015/11/01/go-ahead-get-naked/

http://www.lifechangehealthinstitute.ie/character-defense-structure/

http://theunboundedspirit.com/we-were-made-for-these-times/

http://imaginenoborders.org/pdf/zines/UnderstandingPatriarchy.pdf

http://blog.thespiritualcatalyst.com/the-alchemy-of-fear-and-love/

Let's Get Naked: A Talk about Men, Women and the Erotic Creature — TEDex Talk Sheila Kelley www.youtube.com/watch?v=YFsUv2SDMq8

http://stylelikeu.com/the-whats-underneath-project-2/maybe-im-not-fuckable-thats-fine-im-not-fuck/

Sera Beak on fear, trembling and daring to unleash your soul's true voice as a woman. https://youtu.be/pDmwLLqh7hk

http://departments.kings.edu/womens_history/witch/werror.html

http://www.salon.com/2005/02/01/witch_craze/

Radical Feminism, Mary Daly, http://en.wikipedia.org/wiki/Mary_Daly, https://philosophynow.org/issues/33/Mary_Daly

http://www.junginstitute.org/pdf_files/JungV8N2p11-44.pdf

http://www.theguardian.com/science/2015/aug/21/study-of-holocaust-survivors-finds-trauma-passed-on-to-childrens-genes

http://yogadork.com/2013/08/29/rage-fear-sadness-fatigue-the-yoga-of-darkness

http://www.lessons4living.com/shadow.htm

http://www.rebellesociety.com/2015/02/25/on-loving-a-daughter-made-of-fire/

http://magoism.net/2014/03/31/essay-part-2-gaia-as-universe-earth-self-a-unity-of-being-by-glenys-livingstone-ph-d/

WEBSITES

Dreaming Aloud.net

Gather the Women

ALisa Starkweather.com

The Icarus Project

The Spirit that Moves Me

Rebelle Society

Do it Girl.com

Return to Mago

Rebecka Eggers.com

ABOUT THE AUTHOR

LUCY H. PEARCE is the author of five life-changing non-fiction books for women including the #1 Amazon bestsellers *Moon Time: harness the ever-changing energy of your menstrual cycle* (now in its second edition) and *The Rainbow Way: cultivating creativity in the midst of motherhood.*

Lucy is an award-winning graduate in the History of Ideas. Former contributing editor at JUNO magazine, she wrote her popular column, Dreaming Aloud, for the magazine for almost five years. Her writing has appeared in major book anthologies (Tiny Buddha, BlogHer, Wild Sister), newspapers and magazines around the world. She is much in demand as an inspirational speaker in the field of women's creativity and the menstrual cycle.

You can find out more about Lucy and her work on her website, dreamingaloud.net, along with her art, e-courses, online shop and event schedule.

Lucy is the founder of Womancraft Publishing, which publishes transformational books by women, for women. She lives and works in East Cork, Ireland with her husband and three children.

CONTRIBUTORS

I want to wholeheartedly thank all the writers, organisations and activists I have quoted in this book. The following writers answered my call to share longer creative contributions for which I am extremely grateful:

ALisa Starkweather is the founder of the Red Tent Temple Movement, Priestess Path Apprenticeship, Women's Belly and Womb Conferences, Daughters of the Earth Gatherings and the Women in Power initiations. She is the co-producer of the award winning film *Things We Don't Talk About; Women's Stories from the Red Tent*, co-author of *The Red Tent Movement: A Historical Perspective* and contributor to *Women, Spirituality and Transformative Leadership*. She has worked uniquely with the sacred feminine and empowerment for thirty-two years.
alisastarkweather.com

Isabel Abbott: writer. activist. speaker artist.
sanctuary in birth, sex, and death.
love for the holy and hedonistic hearts.
isabelabbott.com

Shiloh Sophia McCloud is a well-known artist and writer who has authored and illustrated five books and is the founder of Cosmic Cowgirls, LLC. Shiloh has taught at a variety of graduate schools including New College of California, California Institute of Integral Studies, and in the Women's Spirituality department and the Global PhD program at Sofia University, formerly the Institute of Transpersonal Psychology.
shilohsophiastudios.com

Molly Remer, MSW, M.Div, is a teacher, writer, priestess, and artist who plans and facilitates women's circles, seasonal retreats and rituals, mother-daughter circles, family ceremonies, and red tent circles in rural Missouri. Molly is the author of *Womanrunes: a guide to their use and interpretation; Earthprayer, Birthprayer, Lifeprayer, Womanprayer* and *The Red Tent Resource Kit.* Molly and her husband Mark co-create original goddess sculptures and jewellery at Brigid's Grove

brigidsgrove.com

Julie Daley is a leadership coach, innovation catalyst, writer, and speaker. She works with people around the world to awaken their essential nature so they can live into the full expression of their soul's purpose. Julie loves being with her grandchildren and finding grace on the dance floor.

unabashedlyfemale.com

juliedaley.com

Bethany Webster is a writer, transformational coach, international speaker and what you could call a midwife of the heart. Her work is focused on helping women heal the mother wound so that they can fully claim their brilliance, own their power and live as their authentic selves.

womboflight.com

Antonia Rothschild is an Indigo writer, intuitive healer and yoga teacher.

hippieserendipity.wordpress.com

Matt Licata, PhD, is a psychotherapist, spiritual guide and editor of *A Healing Space* blog. He offers retreats, workshops, and private sessions around the world.

mattlicataphd.com

ABOUT THE ARTIST

ROBIN QUINLIVAN lives in Tucker County, West Virginia, USA, where she co-owns an art gallery. She works mainly in oil pastels, and also oil and acrylic paint. She is a former student of Davis and Elkins College and West Virginia University, where she studied Environmental Science.

A fourth generation artist, she has been drawing and painting ever since she can remember, and is mainly self-taught. Found in various publications around the world, her work is inspired by a deep love and admiration for nature and wild things, travels, dreams, and symbolism. She lives in the mountains with her partner, baby daughter, and two draft horses.

The etching 'Waiting To Fly', featured on the cover of *Burning Woman*, is about hope, and the longing to have wings, to lift ourselves above the things that may restrain us.

etsy.com/shop/RobinQuinlivan

Womancraft
PUBLISHING

Life-changing, paradigm-shifting books
by women, for women

Visit us at www.womancraftpublishing.com
where you can sign up to the mailing list and receive
samples of our forthcoming titles before anyone else.

ⓕ Womancraft_Publishing

ⓦ WomancraftBooks

ⓘ WomancraftPublishing

If you have enjoyed this book, please leave a
review with your favourite retailer.

Also from
WOMANCRAFT PUBLISHING

Moon Time: harness the ever-changing energy of your menstrual cycle

by Lucy H. Pearce
ISBN 978-1-910559-06-2

Amazon #1 bestseller in Menstruation.

Hailed as 'life-changing' by women around the world, *Moon Time* shares a fully embodied understanding of the menstrual cycle. Full of practical insight, empowering resources, creative activities and passion, this book will put women back in touch with their body's wisdom.

Whether the reader is coming off the pill, wanting to understand her fertility, struggling with PMS, healing from womb issues, coming back to cycles after childbirth or just wanting a deeper understanding of her body, *Moon Time* is an empowering read.

Lucy, your book is monumental. The wisdom in Moon Time sets a new course where we glimpse a future culture reshaped by honoring our womanhood journeys one woman at a time.

ALisa Starkweather, author and founder of Red Tent Temple

Liberating Motherhood: Birthing the Purplestockings Movement

by Vanessa Olorenshaw
ISBN 978-1-910559-19-2

If it is true that there have been waves of feminism, then mothers' rights are the flotsam left behind on the ocean surface of patriarchy. Mothers are in bondage – and not in a 50 Shades way.

Liberating Motherhood discusses our bodies, our minds, our labour and our hearts, exploring issues from birth and breastfeeding to mental health, economics, politics, basic incomes and love and in doing so, broaches a conversation we've been avoiding for years: how do we value motherhood?

Highly acclaimed by leading parenting authors, academics and activists, with a foreword by Naomi Stadlen, founder of Mothers Talking and author of *What Mothers Do*, and *How Mothers Love*.

Lucid and riveting... This is The Female Eunuch of the 21st century.
Steve Biddulph, bestselling author of *Raising Boys, Raising Girls,* and *The Secret of Happy Children*

Liberating Motherhood is an important contribution to a vital debate of our times. Vanessa Olorenshaw speaks with warmth, wit and clarity, representing lives and voices unheard for too long.

Shami Chakrabarti, author of *On Liberty*, former director of Liberty and formerly 'the most dangerous woman in Britain'

The Heart of the Labyrinth

by Nicole Schwab
ISBN 978-1-910559-00-0

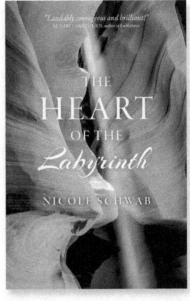

Reminiscent of Paulo Coelho's masterpiece *The Alchemist* and Lynn V. Andrew's acclaimed *Medicine Woman* series, *The Heart of the Labyrinth* is a beautifully evocative spiritual parable, filled with exotic landscapes and transformational soul lessons.

As everything she thought she knew about herself disintegrates: her health, career, family and identity, Maya embarks on a journey of discovery to the land of her ancestors. Coming face-to-face with her subconscious belief that being a woman is a threat, she understands that to step into wholeness she will have to reclaim the sacred feminine fire burning in her soul.

Once in a while, a book comes along that kindles the fire of our inner wisdom so profoundly, the words seem to leap off the page and go straight into our heart. If you read only one book this year, this is it.

Dean Ornish, M.D, President, Preventive Medicine Research Institute, Author of *The Spectrum*

Reaching for the Moon: a girl's guide to her cycles

by Lucy H. Pearce
ISBN 978-1-910559-08-6

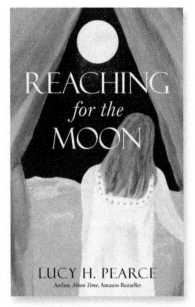

The girls' version of Lucy H. Pearce's Amazon bestselling book *Moon Time*. For girls aged 9-14, as they anticipate and experience their body's changes. *Reaching for the Moon* is a nurturing celebration of a girl's transformation to womanhood.

Beginning with an imaginary journey into the red tent, a traditional place of women's wisdom, gifts and secrets of womanhood are imparted in a gentle lyrical way. along with practical advice.

Now also available in the following translations:

Reiken naar de Maan (Dutch)
Rejoindre la Lune (French)
W Rytmie Księżyca (Polish)

A message of wonder, empowerment, magic and beauty in the shared secrets of our femininity . . . written to encourage girls to embrace their transition to womanhood in a knowledgeable, supported, loving way.

thelovingparent.com

The Other Side of the River: Stories of Women, Water and the World

by Eila Kundrie Carrico
ISBN 978-1-910559-18-5

A deep searching into the ways we become dammed and how we recover fluidity. It is a journey through memory and time, personal and shared landscapes to discover the source, the flow and the deltas of women and water.

Rooted in rivers, inspired by wetlands, sources and tributaries, this book weaves its path between the banks of memory and story, from Florida to Kyoto, storm-ravaged New Orleans to London, via San Francisco and Ghana. We navigate through flood and drought to confront the place of wildness in the age of technology.

Part memoir, part manifesto, part travelogue and part love letter to myth and ecology, *The Other Side of the River* is an intricately woven tale of finding your flow . . . and your roots.

An instant classic for the new paradigm.

Lucia Chiavola Birnbaum, award-winning author and Professor Emeritus

The Heroines Club: A Mother-Daughter Empowerment Circle

by Melia Keeton-Digby
ISBN 978-1-910559-14-7

Nourishing guidance and a creative approach for mothers and daughters, aged 7+, to learn and grow together through the study of women's history. Each month focuses on a different heroine, featuring athletes, inventors, artists, and revolutionaries from around the world—including Frida Kahlo, Rosalind Franklin, Amelia Earhart, Anne Frank, Maya Angelou and Malala Yousafzai as strong role models for young girls to learn about, look up to, and be inspired by.

The Heroines Club is truly a must-have book for mothers who wish to foster a deeper connection with their daughters. As mothers, we are our daughter's first teacher, role model, and wise counsel. This book should be in every woman's hands, and passed down from generation to generation.

Wendy Cook, founder and facilitator of Mighty Girl Art

Moon Dreams Diary

by Starr Meneely
ISBN 978-1-910559-34-5

- 52-week diary
- Space to doodle
- Beautiful illustrations to colour
- Information on charting your cycle
- Learn about the moon's phases and how they affect you
- Quotations to inspire and uplift

This journal will set young women on a path of mindfulness, self-love and connection with the wild, beautiful, natural world around them. It has the potential to be life changing; reclaiming our menstrual cycle as a sacred, powerful experience, rather than the revolting weakness that modern society seems to view it as. Every woman needs a Moon Dreams journal!

Lucy AitkenRead, *Lulastic and the Hippyshake*

Moods of Motherhood: the inner journey of mothering

by Lucy H. Pearce
ISBN 978-1-910559-03-1

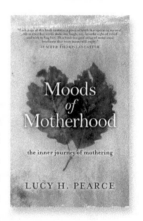

Giving voice to the often nebulous, unspoken tumble of emotions that motherhood evokes: tenderness, frustration, joy, grief, anger, depression and love, Pearce explores the taboo subjects of maternal ambiguity, competitiveness, and the quest for perfection, offering support, acceptance, and hope to mothers everywhere.

Lucy's frank and forthright style paired with beautiful, haunting language and her talent for storytelling will have any parent nodding, crying and laughing along – appreciating the good and the bad, the hard and the soft, the light and the dark. A must-read for any new parent.

Zoe Foster, *JUNO* magazine

Full Circle Health: integrated health charting for women

by Lucy H. Pearce
ISBN 978-1-910559-222

FULL CIRCLE HEALTH
· integrated health charting for women ·

LUCY H. PEARCE

Welcome to *Full Circle Health*. A creative approach to holistic health for all who love planners, trackers and bullet journals to guide and support you in a greater understanding of your physical, mental and emotional health.

Whether menstruating or not, pregnant or post-partum, *Full Circle Health* provides a highly flexible, deeply supportive way of tracking your health, whatever your current health conditions.

Find guidance on:

• Cycles and why they are important for women's health
• Health charting a variety of physical and mental health conditions
• Menstrual charting
• Lunar charting
• Dream charting
• Guided journaling

With 35 daily charting spreads, a monthly habit tracker, planner, and charting grid, this integrated tool will help you to track symptoms, medication, self-care, energy levels, build positive health habits and mindful awareness.

Dirty & Divine: a transformative journey through tarot

by Alice B. Grist

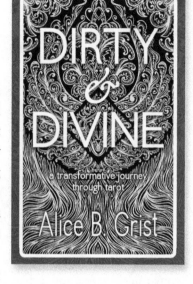

There is something sacred within you, in all that you are and all that you do. In a mix of you that is everyday dirty, and spiritually divine, there is something so perfect, something more. Welcome to your journey back home; to your dirty, divine passage back to you.

Wherever you are, whether beginner or seasoned tarot practitioner, *Dirty & Divine* is written for you, to accompany you on a powerful personal intuitive journey to plumb the depths of your existence and encompass the spectrum of wisdom that the cards can offer.

Dirty & Divine is a tarot-led vision quest to reclaiming your femininity in all its lucid and colourful depths.

Alice has been my go-to woman for tarot readings for years now, because her truth, knowledge + wisdom are the REAL DEAL.
Lisa Lister, author of *Love your Lady Landscape*

The Goddess in You

by Patrícia Lemos and Ana Afonso

The Goddess in You is especially created for girls aged 9-14 years, offering a unique, interactive approach to establishing cycle awareness, positive health and well-being. It contains thirteen beautifully designed cycle mandalas, each illustrated with a goddess from Greek mythology.

Easy to understand and attractive to use, this powerful book celebrates what it means to be a girl growing into womanhood.

- 13 double-sided cycle mandalas illustrated with goddesses

- Instructions for use

- An introduction to the 13 featured Greek goddesses

- A basic, age-appropriate introduction to the menstrual cycle

- Self-care tips for health and well-being

A beautiful resource... Both psychologically sophisticated and delightfully simple to use, I warmly recommend this book to girls, parents and schools.
Jane Bennett, author of *A Blessing Not a Curse*

A simple and beautiful invitation to help girls build a relationship with their menstrual cycle. We highly recommend this book for all young menstruating women.
Alexandra Pope and Sjanie Hugo Wurlitzer, co-authors of *Wild Power*

CPSIA information can be obtained
at www.ICGtesting.com
Printed in the USA
BVHW03s1147250718
522625BV00001B/24/P

9 781910 559161